T0078329

THE
FAIR
DINKUM
ECONOMY

Changing Direction for a Brighter Future

ROBERT GIBSON

For book orders, email orders@traffordpublishing.com.sg

Most Trafford Singapore titles are also available at major online book retailers.

Printed in Singapore.

ISBN: 978-1-4669-9140-8 (sc)
ISBN: 978-1-4669-9141-5 (hc)
ISBN: 978-1-4669-9142-2 (e)

Library of Congress Control Number: 2013909229

Trafford rev. 05/14/2013

TrÆfford   www.traffordpublishing.com.sg

Singapore
toll-free: 800 101 2656 (Singapore)
Fax: 800 101 2656 (Singapore)

"To my children, Mark, Peter, Katherine and Emma,
my grandchildren, Evangeline and Bethany
and to all future generations."

CONTENTS

PREFACE

At one point in 2002, when I started writing this book, I thought to myself *who the hell am **I** to be telling the World's leaders how they should be running their countries.* Then, as I researched further, and came to realise the extent of the shit-hole state our countries are in, I figured, *well Robert, regardless of however out-there and crazy your ideas may seem, they cannot be much worse than those of the current mob of decision makers.*

People need to be encouraged to present their ideas—debate is healthy. New ideas stimulate thinking along different lines, about different possibilities. A new idea may evolve into a workable solution which has little resemblance to the original proposal, but without the initial idea, the solution may never have been considered. For this reason I welcome criticism, like a mistake, we can learn from it, and often end up with a better result, and become a better person/society because of it.

Good companies value their employees, good companies look after their customers, good companies are proud of their products, good companies are good corporate citizens, and good companies protect the environment. An ideal world would be one made up of good companies—alas they are few and far between.

In 2002, I was working for an engineering company in Australia. Many businesses were suffering from competition from overseas imports. It was clear that we could not be competitive with other countries that paid wage rates less than 10th of ours. At that time, these Developing Countries did not have our level of skills and quality control, but I realised, as did most managers and workers that it was only a matter of time before they caught up, and decimated our manufacturing sector. Over the last 10 years, we have watched with frustration and dismay as our prediction came to be.

This started me thinking about the problems with Globalisation and ways to improve the system to prevent what I saw as the inevitable decline in the standard of living in Developed Countries. The inaction of governments was deafening, either they did not want to admit they had got it wrong or they did not know what to do about it. After a lot of consideration, I formulated a rough idea of a possible way to prevent what was happening, and try to improve the situation for all concerned. I decided to write a book to share my thoughts, and hopefully stimulate discussion. At first I concentrated just on this issue and developments over the last 40 years, but as time passed it became obvious that the root of the problem went much deeper. I traced the cause back to the start of the Industrial Revolution and the Free Enterprise System, 250 years ago. I therefore decided, to widen the scope of my book, to include this period.

The more I thought about the economic problems, the more complex they became. I found myself also thinking about the associated social and environmental problems. There is a strong relationship between all these issues, so I decided to include chapters on these relationships, where the economic issues impacted on the non-economic ones.

We all do our bit in our little corners, and together it makes the World go around. It is impossible for any one person to understand all the complexities of modern day business and finance, but to me it is blatantly obvious that the current system is not working. What I am offering is a new perspective which may start people thinking about alternatives they had not previously considered.

I did not want to write a dry academic textbook, full of statistics with complex hypothesises and deductions. I have tried to write at a basic level, so it can be understood by all people as I feel a change if it is to happen, will require the support of those most affected by the shortcomings of the current system—the 90%, struggling majority of the population. Our economic system affects our jobs, our self-esteem, our happiness, the environment we live in, the quality of the goods we buy, our security, and the state of the world we leave to our children. In writing this way, I run the risk of not being taken seriously by the professional community, but it is my belief that the best way forward often gets lost in a sea of political and academic argument. I hope, by using real examples and common sense as the basis for my proposals, to appeal to a wider community, and receive greater support.

There are many academics better qualified to talk about economic theory than I, but many of them do not have any practical experience, and work in institutions and offices far removed from the everyday realities of life. What I feel I have to offer to this discussion is a combination of skills which bring a fresh perspective to the current theories. These are:

- I am a qualified management accountant.
- I have worked for 45 years in a variety of industries, heavy manufacturing, engineering, retail, education, law and farming.
- I have been responsible for the computer installations in most of the companies I have worked.
- I was born in 1949, and have experienced firsthand the development of all of the problems that I have discussed in this book (one of the few benefits of growing old).

I do not believe in criticising something unless you have an alternative suggestion to offer. What follows is a skeleton of my ideas for a new system which I feel has the promise of a new and better model. This skeleton will need a lot of fleshing out, but I am confident, given a chance, it can be brought to life.

INTRODUCTION

I feel that, at the moment, the World is like a ship in a massive storm; we are not sure what is to come or how bad it will be. We would like to turn around and run back to safe waters, but we have to keep facing into the waves for fear of being swamped. We are just hoping and praying that things will not get much worse, and that our fragile craft will hold together. Let me tell you, I do not think the storm will ever end if we stay on our current course!

What is it about the human race, why do we always seem to wait until things have gone too far, sometimes irreversibly before we do anything about it! We wait for the ice caps to melt before getting serious about global warming, we wait until water and electricity prices really start to hurt before we become frugal in their use, dictators are deposed by revolution because they refused to change their ways, animal species disappear while we are still talking about how to protect them, rivers get so polluted they become lifeless drains before we truly get concerned, people get seriously ill before they decide to lose weight or stop smoking . . . . are we currently seeing this flaw in our behaviour in regard to Globalisation? If this was a fire, we would quickly react, as soon as we heard the alarm—the Globalisation fire has started, let's not wait until the house is ablaze.

Mankind is at a crises point, many long-established industries in Developed Countries are in decline. This is the result of the free trade between nations, which has been promoted by Governments over the last 30 years. Whilst in the short term this appears to be good for the Developing Countries it will eventually backfire. Developing Countries rely on the Developed Countries to buy their goods, and as the latter's standard of living declines so too will their buying power. Developed Countries are not about to sit back and let this happen.

In my own country, Australia, I have seen the demise of many of our long-established, core industries such as clothing, electronics, car and steel manufacturing. Most of our agricultural sectors are under threat and in decline. Industries that once employed hundreds of thousands of skilled workers have collapsed, and this trend shows no sign of abating. In June 2012, the Prime Minister of Australia made a startling, but hardly surprising, statement to Parliament, when announcing government cut-backs, to one of their remaining protectionist policies. The following is an extract . . .

"There is not much we can do in Australia any more that can compete on the world market". "We've had to bow out gracefully from most industries, and sadly, despite this government's best efforts; we cannot keep throwing good money after bad".

Capitalism has proved to be the best economic system for the World for the last 200 years. It has allowed the people living in Developed Countries to escape the abject poverty and disease which typified the lives of nine tenths of society in the early 19th Century. From an economic perspective, its main strengths has been in encouraging individuals to strive to improve themselves, and in providing everyone the opportunity to have a better standard of living—if they are willing to work for it. Unfortunately, it has also encouraged greed. From what I see, people are putting a lot more emphasis on material possessions, and are becoming exceedingly self-centred. I think the media and marketing have played a large part in this in putting pressure on consumers to "keep up with the Joneses", people start to feel inadequate if they do not have the latest and greatest car, TV, clothes, house etc. This has led to increased stress in the community, the development of a disposable mentality and a strong growth in the level of debt in Developed Countries. Capitalism has been continually evolving over the decades, but some of the changes have detracted from its original purpose and intention. Most of these changes have been attempts by Governments to control the market to achieve specific economic goals, but big business has also sought to control and modify the system to enable them to better achieve their aims, some of which have not been all that noble.

Quality goods are an endangered species. The theory was that competition would result in an improvement in the quality of goods sold, but this certainly has not proven to be the case, in fact, as far as international competition is concerned, it has been just the opposite. I am fed up with buying imported shirts whose stitching falls apart and the colours fade after two or three washes, knives that do not hold an edge, supermarket-home brand breakfast cereal, and chocolate where the box tastes better than the contents, and the list goes on and on. This lack of quality is not just confined to basic consumer goods, I have seen and heard of many problems with things like concrete cracking, steel breaking, and components for trains which do not fit the design, electrical items catching fire, car components failing, all when they should work perfectly and last for many years. What can be done to stem this decline? Free trade is certainly resulting in cheaper products, but of lesser quality—is this way for the betterment of mankind? I believe that ultimately this will be to the detriment of both Developed and Developing Countries.

Globalisation has accelerated the use of the World's limited resources. It has encouraged our ever-increasing demands for power to fuel industry, our insatiable need for material possessions, and our wasteful use of non-renewable resources. These consequences combined with the world's failure to curb global population growth, if allowed to continue, will soon lead to critical, life-threatening problems for future generations.

The above problems have been caused directly by Globalisation, but it has also resulted in a number of other serious consequences like the exploitation of workers in Developing Countries, the undesirable side-effects from the growth of large multinational corporations and the negative impact of free trade on our environment.

So what is the answer? Is there a better, fairer way? The Free Enterprise System was created at a time when the World was a much "larger" place, there was no such thing as instant communication, transport was primitive, travel was difficult and expensive, and financial systems were unsophisticated. Computers and the Internet have opened up enormous possibilities, which we should be exploiting, to solve the shortcomings of our antiquated systems. Modern computer technology has given us the tools for vast improvements in running World Trade, but they are not being used to anywhere near their potential. I believe changes over the last 50 years have presented us with the opportunity to increase the sophistication of the system, and solve many of its current economic shortcomings.

The first part of this book discusses the shortcomings of Capitalism, the Free Enterprise System, Protectionism and Globalisation. I am not proposing that we scrap the Free Enterprise System; I believe it is a powerful concept, and its aims are still highly relevant, the problem is it has been hijacked by PRICE, and this is the main cause of the dilemma we find ourselves in today. There is more driving free enterprise than just price, but the price has become the only determinant in many people's buying decisions. How do we get the focus back on other qualities like quality and service?

The latter part of this book covers my proposals for improvements. What I am proposing is perhaps the most radical change the Free Enterprise System has undergone, a change to its fundamental principles. In Australia, the term "fair dinkum" is a colloquialism for something which is honest and fair. If a person is fair dinkum, then they are considered by their peers to be someone you can trust, true to their word, someone who will do the right thing by you. If a deal is fair dinkum, then is it considered to be just what it purports to be without any hidden catches or pitfalls. I have used this term to describe a new economy which treats all people fairly; it rewards people for their efforts, and does not take advantage or exploit those who are less fortunate. It is intended for a world that encourages and compensates hard work, and still has incentives for those entrepreneurs who are willing to take risks to build a better future for themselves.

Now these may sound like rather dull and boring topics, and your first reaction is probably that these are things that do not really concern you as you do not have any influence over them, but you are wrong. The operation of our economic system effects everyone's daily life, and like the quality of the air you breathe, you can do something, no matter how small, to improve it if you seriously try; if you do nothing things will just continue to get worse. It is not possible to eliminate greed, but what I have aimed for is a system which tries to ensure an individual's rewards are not at the expense of others. I have tried to think of a way to raise the standard of living in underdeveloped countries without destroying those of the current leading nations. We need to learn from our experience, we should study the pros and cons of our current model, and keep the good, but modify it to overcome the destructive. This is the essence of this book.

THE FREE ENTERPRISE SYSTEM (FES) EXPOSED

The Free Enterprise System (FES) started about the time of the Industrial Revolution, a couple of hundred years ago. Prior to this people lived a subsistence lifestyle based around agriculture, small-scale manufacturing and trade. The Industrial Revolution gave them a means of mass-producing consistent-quality products that vastly increased their profit potential. Capitalism quickly grew as individual wealth increased. Countries that were early adopters of mechanisation soon came to dominate world trade.

The world needed a way of deciding the relative price of goods, and the FES was the answer. Market forces set the price of goods based on supply and demand for a product or service. In theory it is a good system provided there is a healthy level of competition and consumers, at the time of buying, have a good knowledge of all the competing prices, at the time they are buying, but this is rarely the case in reality. This system was based on a few basic assumptions—consumers can distinguish between the various quality of goods; competition leads to cheaper prices; competition will result in an improvement in the quality of goods and services; the best companies will survive. Originally, in small communities, where everyone bought locally, and knew the farmers, shopkeepers, and factory owners, and there were only a few stable brands of each product, this system probably worked well.

In today's world, the FES falls far short of its original ideals. It is not perfect because people are not perfect, there will always be greedy people who are keen to exploit a system to their advantage, and innocent victims who will suffer as a consequence. For all its good the FES has a dark side, it is based on competition and winning at the expense of others. It makes people very self-centred and selfish. The last 50 years have seen the rapid growth of global companies; these companies have become tremendously powerful, and that power is too often abused to build their own empires and returns to shareholders, at the expense of the greater community. We have seen many of these large multinational conglomerates buying up their competition to eventually dominate the market. They often become the only significant buyer for many of their components and raw materials, and this is an extremely dangerous situation as it exposes the market to exploitation where buyers can force raw material prices below what is sustainable. This can lead to the downfall of their suppliers. We have seen this happening in all markets; in agriculture (e.g. sugar, wheat, wool, dairying, meat, vegetables, and fruit), mining (e.g. coal, nickel, and iron ore); textiles; printing and manufacturing. What we have also seen is companies downsizing local operations, and relocating overseas even though they are making record profits. In underdeveloped countries, we see struggling families working for large multinational corporations for a few dollars per week, and countries selling their precious resources or produce for a few percent profit while their people live in poverty.

On 20ᵗʰ February 2013, the ANZ bank in Australia (one of the largest) announced it was cutting 70 jobs from its wealth management operations and outsourcing the work to India; this came the week after announcing a quarterly profit of $ 1.36 billion, and being on track for a record annual profit. The next day Telstra (Australia's largest telecommunications company) announced it would sack 648 jobs from its Yellow Pages Division; 257 of these were due to a drop in advertising in its print business, but 391 were jobs which were outsourced to The Philippines and India. This came shortly after announcing a record half-year profit of $1.6 billion . . . . and more jobs cuts are expected!

The growth in international trade in the middle of the 20ᵗʰ Century started to hurt local industries in Developed Countries. They cried out for their governments to act to protect their markets. This resulted in the introduction of a high level of trade-restrictions such as tariffs, quotas, and embargoes as well as a number of government subsidies to local producers. Starting in the 1980s, governments of Developed Countries yielded to external pressure, and started to open up their markets to free trade; this became known as "Globalisation". Over the last 30 years, this policy has caused a lot of damage to the manufacturing and agricultural sectors in these countries. They are now faced with a critical problem—how do they stop the damage to their economy and the decline in their standard of living. All countries have now become so dependent on world trade that Developed Countries are not game to return to the days of protectionism, for fear it will have a fatal effect on the World's economies.

During the second half of the 20th Century, we saw a number of companies eliminating competition to the extent that they came to dominate their market. Some of these companies exploited their position by driving down the price they pay their suppliers, and inflating the price they charge their customers. It was soon obvious that private industry could not be trusted to self-regulate, and that the forces of demand and supply could not control the price in such circumstances, so governments had to intervene. This resulted in the introduction of anti-monopoly legislation designed to stop one, or a few large companies, from dominating a market segment. Today the term "Free Enterprise" has become a misnomer; companies have had to accept many restrictions over various aspects of their business. Various restrictive trade practice laws have been passed to stop monopolies from forming, to prevent companies colluding to fix prices, to outlaw misleading advertising, and to protect other companies and the public against insolvent trading (i.e. businesses continuing to operate when they knew that they could not pay their debts). In addition to this many other pieces of legislation were passed governing safety standards, environmental controls and employment regulations. Unfortunately, there was always some businessman quick to exploit any shortcomings in the legislation. Each time governments moved to block an abused loophole, someone would find a way to get around it or find another loophole. This would lead to more legislation, and so on. Over the years this has resulted in a system which is highly complex and difficult to enforce, governments have struggled to achieve their objectives, and much time and money is spent trying to police these laws.

We have seen the downfall of the Communist System in Europe where industry was entirely under government control, so we know full regulation does not work, but there is certainly a need for some government intervention.

Due to the uncertainty of what the future holds companies in Developed Countries have become extremely reluctant to invest in new facilities and equipment or even to update their out-dated equipment. Near my home town, a company called Volgren won a government contract to build buses, they did the right thing, bought suitable land, and built a purpose-built factory. They invested heavily in equipment and training of employees, anticipating a long-term return on their investment. Three years later, when the contract was up for renewal, it was awarded to a competitor in another city—the factory now stands idle.

Our insatiable demand for material possessions is also causing an alarming decrease in savings and rising personal debt. In Australia, the Bureau of Statistics records shows that savings decreased from 15.9% of GDP in 1960 to 7.9% in 2010. Personal debt has risen to 100.04% of the annual Gross National Product, the first time it has ever exceeded GNP. Household debt (including mortgages) raised sixfold from 1990 to 2008, well exceeding the consumer price index which only increased by 56% in that period. The trend is the same in the United States and the United Kingdom.

When a business tries to increase its profit it is usually at the expense of their suppliers or customers, why cannot they be happy with just a "reasonable" return on their investment? Consumers are becoming just as hurtful, they are no longer loyalty to the one store, if they can buy an item for 10% less at the new shopping centre down the road then they will. They soon desert their local shop which may have been serving them well for many years. The public is being conditioned (and even encouraged by some firms) to haggle and push the price down as low as possible. This might appear to be good for the customer in the short term, but for businesses, already facing tight margins, it can send them broke, and this is to nobody's benefit in the long run.

Is Competition Really a Good Thing?

In 1981, my wife and I opened a retail shop in a brand new, small shopping centre in Newcastle. Prior to doing this we attended a seminar which was offered by the local university. I was astounded to see the statistics on small business failure in Australia. Their survey showed that 90% of small businesses closed within five years, most of them because the owners go broke. This should have scared us off, but we foolhardily thought (probably as many do) we would be one of the fortunate 10%, and went ahead regardless. We signed a lease for 3 years along with all the other tenants then watched as one by one, 60% of the shops closed before their 3 years was up; some had not even lasted 12 months—it was soul-destroying to witness. After 3 years we moved to cheaper premises in another suburb, but closed the shop 1 year later as the returns did not justify the time and effort were spending. The problems we encountered were:

- Our lack of marketing expertise, which is not uncommon with many small businesses.

- We continually lost sales to cheaper inferior goods because many customers were not willing to pay for quality.
- We refused to meet unreasonable discounts offered by some of our competitors as we realised the futility of this.
- On some products, we were not able to match the prices offered by the larger stores who, because of their "buying power", were able to sell items at prices cheaper than our buying price.

As this was a small centre, we were part of a close community. We became acutely aware of the problems in retailing, and the heartbreak and despair that many owners suffer; if their business fails they often lose their life-savings and sometimes their house, which they had used to secure a loan to finance the venture.

If you carefully observe any shopping centre, you will be surprised at the rapid and high turnover of shops. It is exciting to see a new shop open, but the story behind the scene is often one of despair; a business that has just failed; previous owners who have gone broke; heartache for many years to come for all concerned. The FES has been disastrous for small business. When it started, its main attraction was that anyone, no matter what their status in life, had the opportunity to start their own business and possibly build an empire. Many outstanding businesses started as a local news sheet, a corner store, one-man building company or trucking company or a family farm, but over the years this has become progressively harder to do. Small business is declining rapidly. Owners have become discouraged at having to work long hours for small returns to line the pockets of large companies. There is no security in small business. A small retailer may have to spend $200,000 in setting up a clothing shop. If they work hard, and manage it well, they should be able to expect to have a good long-term investment, but this is rarely the case today. Is this fair?

The 1960s in Australia saw the start of the discount stores. A friend of mine worked in the white goods industry at the time. She worked for the Gas Company who supplied gas for cooking and heating, and also sold gas stoves and heaters to support their business. She said many consumers would come in to compare products and get all the good advice from her specialist, well trained staff. They then would go to one of discount stores and buy the item for 10% less. Needless to say, her department's sales declined and eventually closed to the detriment of consumers who then had to rely on sub-standard advice from the general retail staff of the discounters. The poor retailer that does all the hard work to assist the customer is abandoned. This does not encourage companies to train their staff nor provide good service or quality.

By discounting, sellers aim to increase profit by increasing the quantities that they sell. In Australia, there are 2 large retail corporations who control the grocery industry. In 2012, they started a new price war using low-priced milk to lure customers. The farmers were being paid 13cents per litre for their milk, which was being sold for $1.00—this was cheaper than 3 years previously. The farmers, the consumers, and the government asked the retailers to stop the discounting as everyone could see it was sending the farmers broke, but they continued for many months, doing a lot of damage to their suppliers' and their smaller competitors' businesses.

The other downside of discounting is the paradox that consumers save money. Many retailers use the old ploy of marking up the "normal retail price" to make the "sale price" look more attractive, and many people seem to believe it. I do not think that customers are that gullible, I think they choose to fool themselves as justification for spending what they really cannot afford. Consumers feel pressured to buy before the sale ends even though they may not actually need (as opposed to want) the item; they simply cannot pass up such a bargain which is at a "never to be repeated" price. This impulsive buying results in the consumer buying more than they really need—come on now, how many shirts, jeans, shoes, handbags do you truly need! Often the consumer uses credit to buy an item. They end up spending more than they would have without the sale, so their bank account is actually worse off than it otherwise would have been.

Prior to World War II, there were hardly any women in the workforce. During WWII women were employed in factories to replace the young men who had joined the armed forces; the female participation rate rose to 32%. When I was young, wives worked at home and looked after the family and their house. When a young woman became pregnant, it was expected, and even required, that she would leave her job and raise her family. Since WWII, the female participation rate has increased to 70%. Mothers take maternity leave for 6 months or a year then it is back to their careers, trying to balance their job and home life as best as they can. This has certainly increased the standard of living of families. We have a lot more possessions, more cars, larger houses, eat out more often, and go on fancier holidays, but there is a trade-off; we have more hectic lives, more stress, and parents have less time with their children. Household incomes in Australia have doubled in the last 30 years which gives the impression that our economic system is producing a higher standard of living, but is it really or is it more to do with the fact that most families now have both parents working? What the long-term effects on society will be is yet to be seen, but personally, I think there is a lot to be said for the simple life.

Garages used to be for cars, but these days, people have so many possessions, the garage is too full of stuff which is rarely used, and the car is on the street. You may think that with the amount of stuff you buy, stores should be doing well. It is ironic, but this growing consumerism is actually leading to their destruction. Consumers have a limited amount of money to spend. The fact that they can afford to accumulate so many possessions can be attributed to the lowering of prices . . . . and quality. It follows that, if prices drop, profit margins follow, so stores have to keep selling more to stay afloat—many eventually go under.

The rapid growth of large multinational conglomerates over the last 50 years has seen a much greater degree of price control over the price of their goods and also the price they are willing to pay for goods and materials they buy. The setting of prices by forces of supply and demand may work well where the two parties are equally matched, but this is rarely the case. In many markets, the buyer is such a significant customer for the much smaller supplier that the supplier has little bargaining power, and is forced to accept the price offered. All too often this price barely covers the supplier's cost. On a larger scale, we see the same domination in international markets where the prices of things like coal, sugar, and minerals from smaller or developing countries are determined by large business or governments of the leading Developed Countries. For 20 years, the large supermarkets have been selling their own "home-brands" at prices substantially below the regular suppliers. These started out to be of poor quality, in plain packaging, so the established producers were not too worried, but they have been improving each year, and it has now reached the stage where there is a home-brand alternative for most lines of groceries. I do not have data on what market share the home-brands now hold, but I know traditional suppliers are scared. We are told the stores can do this because they spend less money on "fancy packaging"—are consumers really that gullible? The truth is the lower cost is achieved by either cutting quality or coercing suppliers to reduce their prices. Some suppliers started producing home-brands on behalf of the supermarkets—I am sure they are regretting it now!

The free enterprise system does not work well for farmers. In the good times, there is an overabundance of produce which drives the prices down; in the bad times they cannot produce enough to make a living. There are very few years when the planets line up and they can actually celebrate. Fifty years ago if you owned a farm in Australia, and managed it well, you could expect to make a good living for yourself and your family, but not these days; farmers are being forced to sell to repay mortgages. In a society with a living standard like Australia, farmers should be financially secure and have comfortable lifestyles. The price they are paid for their produce should be sufficient to make sure they drive good cars, they can replace machinery, practice sustainable farming, maintain their buildings, educate their children, put some aside for a rainy day, and still have some left over for some of life's little luxuries. This is not too much to expect for people who risk everything and work as hard as this sector of the workforce does. They own the majority of Australia's land yet in many cases they cannot even scratch out a basic living. Prices for sugar can double or halve over a year, how can you run a business with that much uncertainty. Farmers in Australia get paid 20 cents per kg for corn which ends up costing consumers $12.00 per kg for corn flakes in the supermarket. We have seen many cases where crops have been left to rot on the tree or in the ground as it costs more to get them to market than it is worth. In 2009, I was visiting a friend in New Zealand who owns a small dairy farm; they were selling their newly weaned calves to market for $ 2.00 per head. She told me this was less than the value of the milk that the mother had used to raise the calf. For the last 3 years "cleanskin" wine has been selling in Australia for less than $ 2 per bottle—how can any wine grower be expected to make a living at these prices! For decades now there has been a general migration of farmers to the cities to find work. These people possess great skill and knowledge of agriculture which has been accumulated over many generations, a skill which will now be lost and not passed onto their children. This is a tragedy and a massive loss to any country, a loss which I fear the world will one day come to deeply regret.

The essence of the FES is that competition results in cheaper prices, but we are being blatantly conned by companies who deliberately market the same product under several different brands usually in different price brackets. This is a marketing technique to allow the same product to be sold in different market segments, but it also means many consumers end up paying a higher price for an item that they could have bought cheaper under a different branding. If sometimes, a salesman recommends an item which is cheaper than the well-known brand you enquire about, you can rest assured it is not to help your budget go further, but rather because they make more profit on the cheaper item or they have run out of stock of the expensive brand. The poor consumer is confused, is the cheaper one definitely of the same quality? Do we seriously need all this choice? Do we need to be able to choose between 30 brands of toothpaste (produced by 3 companies) or 20 brands of olive oil— and it is getting worse each decade? Society used to be able to get along without all this choice. Extra brands involve extra cost in branding, packaging, book-keeping, storing and handling. They also take up more shelf space, so we need bigger, more expensive stores.

The Australian consumer group, Choice, carries out detailed tests, comparing similar products from different companies. Each month they analyse and publish results showing consumers how the different brands of various products performed. Their tests often show that some of the cheaper brands perform just as well, if not better than, the expensive ones. Sometimes even with two brands by the same company the cheaper one rates higher. Producers can do their own testing, so why cannot they just do the right thing and use honest prices based on quality and performance—consumers should be able to be rely on the price to determine the quality.

Once the large stores eliminate competition and gain control over the market prices what guarantee do we have that prices will stay down? In Australia, the two largest supermarket chains now own 50% of the petrol stations, and we can already see profit margins increasing on a litre of fuel. With 50,000 items on the supermarket shelves, there is no way you can remember and compare prices between stores especially when they keep changing them so often. Also, think about who is losing when prices are reduced—what is the impact on growers, producers and wholesalers.

Consumers feel ripped-off by shops continually having sales. All sales do is convince consumers that the shops normal price has extremely high margins, so buyers have become accustomed to waiting for "specials" before parting with their money. There is no longer any loyalty; people buy from the cheapest seller.

Consumers may think they are getting a bargain when they get a jumper for half the price of the shop down the road, but what is the real cost of that saving. Everyone has either experienced, or knows of friends, who have suffered from their small business going broke and the owners losing everything they own. The way our world is heading there will be no small businesses. In Australia, many industries like farming, service stations, groceries, butchers, newspaper shops, liquor outlets, paint retailers, hardware stores, and nurseries have been virtually taken over by large business. Is being able to buy six cheap jumpers at half price, as oppose to three quality ones at a higher price, really worth the financial devastation and heartache it causes in our community? If you buy a belt and it cracks two months later, if you buy socks and they make your feet sweat, and you get a hole in the heel after three months, if you buy a drill that is not powerful enough to drill through dry hardwood, is that a bargain? As a society, what we have to decide is, do we want to live in a world without the small, personalised, family businesses that we have all grown up with and love!

And it is not just the small shops that are closing it is also large businesses like builders, hardware chains, food chains, restaurants, service stations etc. When businesses this size fail, the effect is widespread. As well as the distress and financial pain it inflicts on their employees, they often go broke owing many hundreds of thousands, sometimes millions of dollars to their suppliers, with little chance of debt recovery.

In 1998, a highly successful family clothing store in my town closed its doors and laid off 400 workers as it could not compete with cheaper imports. Rundles had made tailor-made suits and other clothing for over 100 years. A similar story was to be found in Victoria where Fletcher Jones was forced to close in 1997. It had operated since 1924, and had grown to be a national entity employing 3,000 workers, one of the largest in the World. These sad stories are typical of what we see in the news every week.

The airline industry is a prime example of the failure of the FES, over the last 20 years we have seen ticket prices tumble, discount fares are readily available which are 80% less than what they were in the 1990s. Some seats (usually corporate and last-minute) are sold at the full price, but many are heavily discounted—"to fill the plane", we are told. This price war has seen the collapse of many airlines worldwide some of them were previous leaders in the industry (e.g. Pan America, Ansett, Eastern Airlines, Delta Air Lines, Northwest Airlines, United States International Airline, Canadian Airlines). In Australia, 73 domestic airlines went broke in the last two decades, in the United States 100 airlines declared bankruptcy in just 20 years. In Europe it is a similar story, Governments have had to try and prop up their country's airlines, but even so there were a lot of casualties like Swissair and Crossair. In Australia in 2012, our largest airline, Qantas, announced it was cutting another 400 engineering jobs, this is on top of 600 engineers it laid off earlier in the year. This is necessary, we are told, due to more competition and falling profits; its share price dropped 25%.

From my observations, the number of flights being delayed and cancelled due to problems with their equipment, is on the increase. Passengers stranded at airports due to the failure of a computer booking system is also becoming a common sight. This is a considerable inconvenience and worry to customers—is this the price they have to pay for cheap flights? You have to ask yourself, what corners are being cut in reducing costs . . . . is it in the training of pilots, airport staff and ground crews or less preventative maintenance—what will be the result of engineering jobs being transferred to Developing Countries? Common sense would tell you this level of discounting is not sustainable in the long term. Why cannot the various parties get together and agree to stop this ridiculous price-war?

Sport is supposed to be the epitome of competition, have you noticed how many sports are controlled to make the game more competitive; in golf you are given a handicap of strokes; in horse racing you are given a handicap of weight; in football there are dollar limits, "caps", on how much you can pay players to stop rich clubs from buying up all the good players; in car, and motorbike racing there are restrictions on the equipment, and engine capacities you are allowed to use; in yacht racing they put the competitors into classes to give the smaller boats some chance of a win; in cricket, and football they put the players into grades for the same reason. This has become necessary over the years to stop the game from effectively becoming a "one or two horse race". Yet in business, it is "dog eat dog"—every man for himself.

We encourage our children to play competitive sport. In doing so, are we fostering an undesirable habit? Are we inadvertently sending them the message that life is all about winning, regardless of the effect on others? Does this make them more self-centred? In sport and most games there are winners and losers, but many more losers than winners; we are so busy celebrating with the winners that nobody gives much thought to the poor losers. I am sure these experiences influence their attitudes later in life when they start making decisions that affect their business, that of their business partners, and competitors. Prior to the 1960s, children led a hugely different lifestyle. They usually had to work from an early age—in my youth, from 8 to 15 years of age, I washed cars, mowed lawns, had a paper run, deliveries pharmaceuticals for a chemist, and helped my father with his milk run; from 15 to 18 years of age I worked in shops and on a delivery truck in the school holidays. My friends and I had neither television (until I was about 14) nor computers, so we made our own fun. We had to be creative making many of our toys out of pegs, cardboard and bits of wood. We rode our bikes 12 kilometres (round trip) to school, walked 4 kilometres (round trip) to the beach in Summer, listened to the radio, went fishing, and occasionally went to the movies of a weekend. We played cricket, football, cards and board games, but it would not have been for more than a few hours per week. We had to manually wind our watches, and polish our school shoes too—we did not have much spare time. Children today have a lot more discretionary time, a lot of it spent on competitive activities. For instance in the 1980s my children and their friends would have easily spent 20 hours each, per week, playing sport, thumping away at computer games, watching TV, and going to the movies. Competitive sport and games are also the themes of many TV shows and movies they watch.

There is a lot of uncertainty that businesses face, much of which they have little control over; like, interest rates, Government regulations, the cost of materials, and goods they sell, the weather, theft, natural disasters, competitors moving into their territory, and of course their own health issues. Is it any wonder failure is so prevalent? Would not it be good to remove some of this risk?

Let us then look in summary at the negative impact of the FES to see how fair it really is. Is it right that:-

For business:

- Manufacturers have to take their manufacturing off-shore in order to survive?
- Farmers have to sell their farms as they have become no longer viable?
- 9 out of 10 new businesses close in the first 5 years?
- Large companies can engage in price wars in order to put smaller competitors out of business?

- Larger businesses have so much negotiating power that they can sell an item for less than smaller businesses can buy the item?
- Sub-contractors and suppliers are left out of pocket when businesses fail?
- Some countries can "dump" (sell their products at less than the usual market price) their excess produce on other nations, and destroy their local producers in the process?

For workers:

- Workers in developed countries have to accept lower-skilled jobs or are forced to retrain because their old jobs have been moved off-shore?
- Workers have to fight continually for wage increases?
- Workers have unpaid entitlements when companies go broke?
- Farmers are amongst the lowest paid workers?
- Lower income families pay a higher percentage of their wages in tax than the high-rollers?
- It is increasingly difficult for low income earners to escape the "poverty trap"?

For the environment:

- Companies and countries continue to pollute our land air, and waterways because it costs "too much" to be environmentally-friendly?

- Forests are being cleared at an ever increasing rate to make way for farming and cities to grow threatening wildlife, and endangered flora?
- Air and water pollution, which has such a global impact, is left to individual countries to control?
- Non-renewable resources are used to make goods with built-in obsolescence, which are designed to have a short lifetime, and have to be replaced continuously?
- We waste enormous quantities of fuel and energy in transporting goods unnecessarily around the World?
- So much paper can be wasted on junk-mail?
- All countries still allow non-sustainable business practices to happen?

For Consumers:

- Is the reduction in the quality of goods we buy and the enjoyment we get from using these goods, worth the savings from cheaper prices?
- As reported in The Age newspaper, in 2009 there were 36,487 cases of personal insolvency in Australia (mainly involving bankruptcy, but also includes debt agreements). Many of these were due to business failure, so this is no small problem. How much do we pay in higher taxes to cover the intangible costs that result from business failure like the legal costs of bankruptcy, unemployment benefits when businesses fail, medical costs brought about by stress, and the tragic increase in suicides?
- When businesses fail they often do so owing large sums to the government, to their landlords, to their bank, to their suppliers, and to their sub-contractors. This

increases the overheads for these organisations and results in an increase in their prices; so other businesses and consumers end up paying more for their goods and services?

Morally:

- Countries go to war over resources?
- You buy an item for which workers in undeveloped countries have been paid a few dollars per day to produce, often in appalling conditions?
- Our generation uses up valuable resources at ever-increasing rates?
- We continue to use non-renewable resources to produce energy simply because "it is cheaper"?
- 80% of world-consumption is by 20% of the population?

Makes you wonder does not it!

Do not let Quality become a Dinosaur

Consumers are not able to determine the quality of many items, and often buy cheap rubbish, which ends up costing them much more than alternative higher priced items. The current system takes advantage of consumer ignorance, to sell a confusing array of poor quality goods to a gullible market.

Most countries of the World now have consumer protection laws that state that goods have to be "fit for purpose" or words of similar meaning. What does "fit for purpose" mean? If you buy a 60 watt light bulb and it provides 60 watts of illumination when you switch it on, is this the end of the manufacturer's responsibility? No, absolutely not! There must also be an intention that it will last for a certain minimum number of hours and provide 60 watts of light consistently during this time. Should this not be the same for all products sold? Consumers should be able to expect goods to last for a reasonable period and perform to an acceptable level during that time. Caveat Emptor ("let the buyer beware")—this principle is at the core of the FES. It protects the seller rather than the ignorant buyer— what a ridiculous concept. How many people even read contract conditions let alone understand them.

If Globalisation is working, we should by now be able to buy goods of equal quality to what we used to make ourselves, at a substantially lower price, but as you will have observed this is not the case. We can certainly buy much cheaper goods, but in many cases they are rubbish—good quality Australian goods are being replaced by cheap rubbish. That is not to say that there are no quality products made in Developing Countries, there are good companies, but they are far outnumbered by the poor quality ones. This turns consumers' minds against all imports from that country. Now, our Government might argue that the proliferation of cheap and nasty goods is the consumers' fault for not being more discerning, but it is not that simple—how can the average consumer tell the difference between the quality of material and thread on a $10 shirt compared to a $100 one. A $40 pair of shoes may look as good as a $120 pair, but only last a quarter as long. The Government has to accept responsibility to protect consumers.

Even when consumers know they are buying rubbish they still continue to do so. You only have to look at the growth of the "bargain" stores (like Golo, Clints, Dollar Dazzlers, $2 Shop, Base, The Reject Shop) over the last decade to realise that many consumers need protecting from their cheap-bargain obsession. Invariably if you buy something cheap it does not do its intended job well nor does it last. You would think, if you buy a cheap travel bag, and the zip breaks half way through your trip, or you buy a cheap tyre, and it has poor grip, and only lasts for 20,000 kilometres, or you buy cheap scissors that chew through material instead of cutting, that you would soon learn not to make the same mistake again.

FES theory is based on the assumption that consumers will not repeat their purchase of brands with which they are not happy. If we were talking about local companies selling into the domestic market, as was the case up to 1970, then this might be right. Back then there were only several Australian companies for each type of product and they had to be good, or their reputation would suffer, word would quickly spread, and people would not buy their products, but when you are dealing with global markets the same laws do not apply. Australian consumers are faced with a huge variety of brands from companies they have never heard of. Local and overseas producers now sell basically the same product under several brand names. The chances are the next time you go to buy a similar item you cannot remember which brand to avoid, and even if you do there will be a good chance you will buy another brand from the same manufacturer (without knowing it), and have the same problem again.

I should not be too critical of consumers' decisions to buy cheaper alternatives as I have done it myself in the past, but I learnt from several bitter experiences (experiences I am sure everyone has had), it is just not worth it. The thing that lures us back to buy another cheap item is that every so often you get a good bargain, a cheap item that actually does what it is intended to do, and we are pleasantly surprised. The question we need to ask ourselves is "do the few good experiences outweigh the majority of bad ones"?—the answer would invariably be NO!

Consumers are missing the joy of owning a quality item. They have to suffer a poor substitute until it either breaks or wears out, or they get so fed up with it they chuck it away. Take, for example, a set of serrated steak knives I bought 6 years ago; they look good and made grand promises about "never needing sharpening", but after about 6 months they started going blunt. From then on they got progressively worse until after 3 years of suffering, I replace them with a quality brand. The quality brand cost three times the price, and if they only lasted for 5 years then I would still be pleased because they have given me joy every day as they glide effortlessly through my meat, pizza, and toast, but I am pretty certain they will last a lot longer than 5 years.

A friend of mine recently had their roof replaced; he went for the cheapest price. In their catalogue, the steel sheets the roofers used looked the same as the locally produced ones and were two thirds the price. He lives close to the ocean, how long do you think these cheap sheets will last? As the material is only 25% of the total cost of the job, they saved 8%. This is false economy as they will invariably have to replace it again, well before they otherwise would have.

I have often heard intelligent friends say things like "Oh, at that price you can just throw it away if it breaks and buy another one"—what a waste of time and resources; they invariably do not enjoy using the item. Another disturbing trend is the buying of a cheap item when you only need to use it once, or infrequently. In the old days, items were built to last and they were expensive, so people used to either borrow from friends, or they would rent the item. Now, because you can buy an item at 1/10 of the price it used to be, people are buying their own. A good example of this was a chain saw a friend of mine bought to cut-up a fallen tree on his property, the cheap steel in the blade had to be sharpened more often, it took longer because of a lack of power, and it was harder to start. Using a good chain saw is a joy, this one did the job, but it was a frustrating experience. My friend admitted he should have just spent the money on a good one, he did not seriously consider renting; are we destroying the rental industry? In buying this rubbish, we are allowing ourselves to be exploited, and sending the wrong message to the manufacturers.

It is not only the high cost of labour that is a problem for developed nations it is also the damage being done to their mindset. For many years now we have been taught that we should be producing quality goods. Governments in all leading countries have encouraged their industries to aim for better quality, do research and development, and build a worldwide reputation for excellence. What are they to do in the face of this cheap competition from overseas? In order to compete, do they throw away these principles, reduce training and research, and start using low-quality materials; is this what the Government wants because that is what they are forcing industries to turn to in order to survive. What will that do to our international trading reputation?

Purchasing officers often make decisions based on price, without taking the service-life of the item into account. I saw this often with the engineering firm where I worked. The buyers, for large customers, who were qualified engineers, and should have known better, would often take the risk and choose an inferior product at a saving of say 5% to 20 % below our price, using material sourced in Asia, without any thought about the service-life of the items. These products often had inferior steel and welds, and often had to be repaired or retired before what should have been their full term.

There is an enormous hidden and unknown cost with faulty goods. Our consumer laws allow us to return goods which do not fulfil their promises, but many people do not like confrontation, so if it is only a small value item, they just "lump-it". I think unscrupulous companies take advantage of this, and even though they put warranties on their goods they know that most of their dodgy products will never be returned. We know we should take faulty goods back to the supplier but . . . . which supplier (you may have only used the item twice in 6 months, and now cannot remember where you bought it), how far away are they, where is the receipt? It all gets too hard does not it. Let's do another rough estimation—say, for example, the average consumer returns 5 items per year (out of probable 15 faulty ones they buy) for warranty claims. Your typical family car costs about 60 cents per km to run, but most of this is for fixed costs like registration, insurance, depreciation and interest; it costs about 20 cents for variable costs like petrol, and wear and tear.

To return the goods, each trip requires a 10 km round journey costing $2 plus the time you waste, say 1 hour. Therefore 5 trips per year costs $10 plus 5 hours of your time. In Australia there are 15 million consumers (excluding the very young and the infirmed), so we can say based on this conservative assumption it is costing our economy $150 million per year plus 75 million hours of lost time—what a waste! Anyway, if you return it, you may get something just as defective. Many people just choose to fix the fault themselves or throw it away rather than return it.

At the moment, it is up to the buyer to return faulty goods, suffering the inconvenience, and cost. If we improved the quality of goods, then there would be fewer problems in the first place. On those infrequent occasions when goods do have faults. **Companies should take replacement items to the customers home or business rather than as it is now, requiring the customer to return the goods**—this would become part of a seller's service and a key selling point.

I am not saying that all companies in Developed Countries are on the decline nor am I saying that all goods produced in Developing Countries are of low quality. There are good manufactures and producers in every country who are managing to overcome the difficulties of the FES, but they are far too few in number.

Manufactures in Developed Countries are increasingly relying on imported material and components from Developing Countries. Once they start doing this they lose control of their quality, the smallest part can have disastrous consequences if it fails. For example look at the problems we have had with cars over recent years, with accelerators sticking, hydraulic brake lines failing and electrical parts catching fire. In January 2013, all Boeing 787 Dreamliner planes were grounded because of concerns about their batteries catching fire. This was Boeing's latest airline, the first one going to service in October 2011, after years of extensive testing and delays. Grounding a model is an extremely rare event, the problem with the batteries was serious enough, but there had already been a number of previous incidents—cracked cockpit windows, brake problems, electrical failures, and fuel leaks. The cost to a company of having to recall or ground their products is horrendous. A small part which fails might only be worth several dollars, but it can cost hundreds of thousands of dollars to fix if it is part of a machine which is part of a greater process as the entire production line would have to be stopped for several days, the machine dismantled and the part replaced.

"As I hurtled through space one thought kept crossing my mind, every part of this rocket was supplied by the lowest bidder"—John Glenn

In order to minimise this risk, they have to send inspectors to audit the overseas business, to verify the adequacy of their quality control systems, and inspect their goods prior to despatch, to ensure they are getting what they were promised. This is a large expense for these companies, but if they do not do it the cost of correcting defects can be much greater. In my job, I have seen and heard many horror stories of imported materials and manufactured items which had the wrong grade of steel, where minimum tolerances for things like straightness, round, thickness, length, and orientation were not met, where welds were faulty, and where the packaging was inadequate to prevent damage to the goods in transit. These problems have to be corrected by the buyer, this usually means replacement material has to be bought on short notice from local sources or flown in from reputable overseas suppliers at much higher prices. This delays the delivery to customers and damages the company's reputation. The buyer then has to try to get compensation from the original overseas manufacturer—good luck with that!

Have you ever had, like me, electrical items that only last a few years, coffee tables whose legs go wonky after 6 months, tools that bend or break when you apply a bit of pressure, detergent where you need a cupful of liquid to get the dishes clean, teapots that leak, steel wool that pricks your fingers, water bottles that leak, combs that scratch your scalp, belts that crack and break, octopus straps that snap, paper towelling that is about as absorbent as newspaper, cling wrap that does not cling, glue that does not stick, bicycle cranks that break, chocolates you gag on, toys whose wheels fall off, shoes that hurt your feet, and whose soles crack, batteries and light globes that do not last, backpacks whose buckles break on your first hike, sunglasses whose lenses distort the view, and do not filter out harmful ultra-violet light, envelopes that do not stick, paintbrushes whose bristles fall out, noisy cars, and my favourite . . . . pens that do not write, and the list goes on and on. And these examples are not confined to the consumer goods it is happening in all industry sectors.

I bought one of those electronic salt and pepper grinder sets nine months ago, it was a reputable brand and on sale (of course). After only six months the pepper grinder stopped working, I replaced the battery, but no luck. I thought about taking it back to the retailer, but that would have involved a half hour search for the receipt then a half hour return trip to the shop. If they insisted on sending it for repair then I would have been without it for a week or two, and I would have been up for another trip to pick it up. So I took it apart, and found one of the battery terminals was corroded right through. I was pretty mad that this could happen after such a short period of time. I used a bit of initiative, and made up a new terminal with part of a paper clip, and it worked well, but why should I have to take up one hour of my time fixing the darn thing after such a short service life.

Four years ago I bought, what used to be a good brand, electric, leaf vacuum. As it was heavy when fully loaded, it had wheels to make it easier to use. A circlip was used to fasten the wheels to the hub, but it was a flimsy affair, it bent and fell off after about the fourth time I used it, and I lost it in the grass—damn! I tried to find a replacement amongst the spare parts in my garage, but I did not have the right size. I put it to one side intending to either buy another circlip (it probably would have been very difficult to find the correct size) or to find the receipt and return it to the hardware store I bought it from—it is still gathering dust in my garage.

Price is no guarantee of quality. It used to be that you could buy reputable brands and be sure of getting good quality, but with many well-respected brands now being produced by Developing Countries the quality has decreased, and you often end up paying the same price for lower quality (e.g. designer clothes, shoes, sunglasses and handbags). I think everyone would be happy to pay more if they could be guaranteed a minimum standard of quality. Quality is enjoyment that lasts. We need governments to regulate the system by introducing minimum quality standards and enforce them which will protect consumers from their ignorance, and rebuild business confidence in the benefits of quality.

Advertising Waste

Marketing is an extremely essential part of the success of any company, but it is hugely expensive. Grocery chains, hardware stores, toy stores, clothing stores, and electrical retailers, flood our letterboxes, televisions, and newspapers with advertisements. Television advertising, and much of the newspaper/journal advertisements are designed to be persuasive, but also informative, advising potential consumers about new products, product features, and where to buy their product. The direct mail campaigns and much of the web-based marketing, however, are focused on persuading consumers to buy by offering the cheapest price—"if you can find a cheaper price elsewhere we will beat it". This type of advertising is not good for our economy, it manipulates people into believing "price is king", and this becomes their prime incentive to buy. Consumers should base their buying decisions on value-for-money; instead they have been conditioned to find the cheapest (often driving many kilometres to get a "bargain"). In emphasising price as their main selling point, companies are perpetuating price-cutting wars with their competitors, and as I have already pointed out, these are wars where there are no winners.

Just think, if every store was selling an item for the same price, then there would be no need for much of the current advertising—how much would retailers save on junk mail? Let's do another rough calculation—I would say 70% of ads in mail catalogues rely on a price to be the only selling point, so if these were eliminated . . . . say conservatively, in Australia companies spend $10 per household per week, and there are 8 million households, then a 70% reduction would amount to $2.9 billion per year that would be freed up for companies to use for better purposes (like training of employees, better working conditions, research and development, higher wages, better environmental controls). Sellers would have to make their advertising material more informative and useful, and have more skilful and attractive designs. Their marketing campaigns would have to become more imaginative and rely on product differentiation, and persuasion to promote their products.

If we were to eliminate price competition, then service would become a vital differential. Staff would be trained and encouraged to listen carefully when you tell them what you want and have the required knowledge to be able to give you an informed opinion, instead of just pretending they know all about the product. It would be the stores that listened to customers' complaints and acted promptly to remedy any problems that would get the repeat business. Maybe service stations would start cleaning windscreens again! Who knows we might even get "service with a smile"!

Sales—a Merchant's Nightmare

"Sales" (discounting items) are an absolute nightmare for merchants, and yet they are forced to have them to match the competition. The practice of discounting has resulted in customers frequently haggling for a lower price when items are not on sale. If a store owner works on a fixed, average profit margin they can plan how much they need to sell and at what price in order make a reasonable profit, however, if they hold frequent sales, it is extremely difficult for them to know how well they are doing as margins are continually changing. For many retailers, particularly the smaller ones, they only know if they are making a profit or not after a time-consuming and infrequent assessment of their books, so most of the time they are just hoping like mad that it will all work out at the end of the month or year.

Consumers have lost all confidence in the integrity of retailers, they have been conditioned to wait, and only buy when an item is on sale. How often have you bought an item only to find it 20% cheaper in the store down the road or even worse on sale at the same store a week later? Customer loyalty used to be highly sought after, but the continuous use of "sales" has all but destroyed this relationship. Nobody would deny a business a reasonable mark-up on their goods, but when you start to see regular discounting of 40% up to 80% you undoubtedly feel you are being ripped-off when you pay full price.

Sales are based on the often-false principle that even though you make a smaller margin on each item, your turnover increases and you will end up making more total profit. This may work for items which have a large market (e.g. foodstuffs, electrical goods), but not for those with a limited market (e.g. cars, lawnmowers, front doors, carpet) as each household will only buy one item and it will last a long time; the seller may bring a sale forward to an earlier time, but they will be eating into future market demand. Let me take an example, say over the last Christmas period a shoe store sold 200 pairs of a particular shoe for $80 each, at 30% profit, they will have made $4,800 (200 x $24) total profit. They decide for this year they would have a 15%-off sale. What increase in turnover would they need, to make the same profit? They would need to sell 400 pairs ($4,800/$12). Do you really think reducing the price by 15% to $68 would result in a doubling of sales? What happens more often than not is the store has a lesser increase in sales than they need maybe to 300; the manager may be happy as they have substantially increased their turnover, but they probably do not realise the effect on their profit. This example is for just one item, but in reality the store would be discounting hundreds of types of shoes all with different prices and profit margins, so the effect of the sale is complex, and unless they have an exceptionally good computer system for tracking each item they cannot know the true effect on profit until it is too late! For businesses that engage in price negotiation with customers, or offer to "meet competitors' prices", it is even harder to know, the effect this policy is having on their profits. Their discounts and margins would be changing on every transaction.

Businesses all too often get into such a price-cutting war that they end up going broke, and send many of their competitors to the wall in the process. I once worked for an engineering firm; we were often amazed at how often we were beaten on a tender by 10 to 30% by some of our competitors. This usually occurred when the market was depressed and they were anxious to win work. These competitors usually did not stay in business long once they started using this pricing policy. Many business owners and managers do not fully realise the impact on their bottom line, of reducing their normal margin. They are often too focused on increasing sales to meet some budget or target (probably the basis for the manager's bonus).

The After-Christmas Sale used to be the biggest of the year. They were originally used to get rid of stock that was left over from the Christmas period, but over the last 10 years, we have seen Pre-Christmas Sales getting bigger and earlier every year; this is just a price-cutting war. This year I have seen these sales starting in early November with discounts up to 80% below the "normal retail price" on items like jewellery, camping gear, and furnishings—this is crazy! I know the "normal retail price" is usually inflated to make the deal look better, and so do most consumers, so they are just getting at the suckers.

Bulk Buying Discounts out of Control

In the 1900s, Producers, and Wholesalers started offering discounts to trade buyers who bought in larger lots. There was justification for this as the packaging, handling, and freight was cheaper per unit, but somewhere along the line this got out of control, and bulk-buying discounts grew and grew. Initially these would have been around 5 to 10%, but today large, national corporations are demanding much higher discounts. The producers used to be the dominant force in the market, but over the years the buyers have consolidated, and have grown rapidly in size and power. Today the buyers are powerful enough to demand bigger discounts on purchases and are in a strong position to influence the market price. In Australia, for example, 50% to 80% of the food, alcohol, hardware, and petrol markets are now dominated by the two retail giants Woolworths and Coles, and they are currently expanding into the insurance and optical markets. Once companies gain control of a market they can charge higher prices. On 27th January 2013, The Sun Herald reported that, according to the Australian Competition and Consumer Commission, when these two Australian retail giants had first launched large expansions into petrol retailing in 2004, their average revenue from a litre of petrol was 3.4 cents. By last year they were getting 6.9 cents per litre. According to FUELtrac retailers' revenue over this 7 year period went from 0.9 cents to 7.1 cents per litre. In the last 3 years, their share of petrol stations had risen to 50% while the number of independent stations has fallen by 16%.

The same changes are happening throughout the World, in the UK and US it is companies like TESCO and Wal-Mart. In 2006, the second largest US supermarket chains, Albertsons, had to sell its business in the face of competition from discounter Wal-Mart. 650 stores were acquired by Supervalu, and 600 by Cerbus; 400 were then closed.

Bulk-buying discounting is discriminating against the smaller retailers, today their buying price is often less than the large retailers selling price. The day of the convenient and friendly corner-store is over, consumers now have to drive further, take twice as long, and often pay for parking to do their grocery shopping. Small businesses used to offer "free service"; our local service station attendant used to fill up our car, check our tyre pressure, clean our windscreen and offer technical advice ("your front passenger tyre is wearing unevenly", "George can you check my battery I have trouble starting of a morning"); our local grocer used to give credit to regular customers (interest free) until next pay day and offer to carry our groceries to our car; doctors used to do home visits; our butcher used to deliver our meat if we could not get to their shop for some reason; the milkman used to deliver fresh milk to our door before daybreak (before we went to work and the sun had time to warm the bottle); the Sunday papers were delivered to our door, out of the weather— ALL FOR FREE! Every block had a corner-store. Locals used to do regular trips (walking) to the shop and only bought what they needed for the next few days, so a couple of small string bags was all that was required to carry the goods home.

So I ask you, is the modern day shopping experience really progress? Ask any mother (sorry sexist), any parent, that has to search for 15 minutes to find a car park, struggle getting children and strollers in and out of cars, push large trolleys whilst herding their brood across busy car parks, find change for the parking meter, and get wet filling the car with petrol if this is a forward step. If the small shopkeeper could still buy for the same price as the large conglomerates, then I am sure they would still be thriving.

The Challenge of Online Retailing

The recent rise in Online Retailing is threatening to be the biggest change in retailing that the industry has ever faced. Online retailers can operate from anywhere in the World, and have a much lower operating cost. In Australia in 2012, they estimated that 10% of all purchases were made online. Whilst it has advantages it is also the greatest threat that traditional retailing has faced. As it becomes more popular (and it is sure to) stores will be forced to downsize or close and staff will be laid off. This will be a massive cost to the economy. Will shopping malls dotted with empty ghost-stores become a common site?

What are the benefits of online retailing?

- Obviously cheaper prices—since they do not have the cost of renting retail space in expensive shopping centres, and they need fewer staff as there are no face-to-face sales assistants.
- Convenience—consumers can buy from anywhere in the World, and have it delivered to their doorstep in a matter of days. This is particularly convenient for people living in remote areas.
- It is easy to buy hard-to-find items.
- Small manufacturers or growers can sell their wares directly without the expense and risk of setting-up expensive shop-fronts.
- Marketing is much cheaper as it is web-based and can potentially reach hundreds of millions of buyers.

What are the disadvantages?

- Consumers cannot see and feel what they are buying.
- Many consumers like the "shopping-experience", nice stores to look at, coffee with friends, maybe take in a movie, have a meal—a real social occasion.

- There is added risk of fraud and identity theft from using the internet.
- Returning goods that do not fit or break is a hassle and a cost.
- Online sellers usually offer some forms of guarantee like "if not satisfied, return within 30 days, no questions asked", but how many people actually go to the trouble of returning unsatisfactory goods. You have to ring the supplier and explain why you want to return the goods, get a return number, re-package the goods, take it to the post office, or courier, pay the freight, and then wait to get your money back, hopefully including the cost of the return freight.
- Consumers are often not home when the goods are delivered, so there is a risk of theft or spoilage. Otherwise, they have to pick up the parcel from a central depot.
- Having goods delivered to your door involves more packaging and results in many more delivery trucks on the road, increasing traffic congestion, which leads to more damage to the environment?
- The threat to traditional retailing—too many people are going to their local shop, trying on clothes and shoes; getting advice on the best tools to use for a particular task; asking what golf club and size to buy, then going home and buying online—is this practice fair on the poor struggling shop keeper!

Technology is changing retailing, and that offers some real benefits to sellers and buyers. I think there will always be stores for those people who prefer them, but the way things are heading there will be a lesser number of outlets, and maybe they will be of a more basic design. Traditional retailing is fun; would not it be good to be able to accommodate on-line buying without radically changing retailing as we know it?

The changes I have proposed in this book will mean that online selling will lose its price advantage which will certainly slow the growth of that sector, but as I have pointed out above, there will still be a number of strong reasons to buy online, so it is undoubtedly here to stay. Taking away their price advantage may mean that instead of online traders taking maybe a 50% share (who knows) of the retail market they may only get 20% . . . . I believe this would be a good thing.

A few years ago I wanted to buy an electric block-splitter to split wood for my fuel fire. The local shops did not have what I was after, so I went online. I found an Australian website with the style I was after and it looked the part. I bought it (cost $350), it arrived a few days later, it looked very sturdy, heavy gauge steel and a good design. It worked fine the first time I used it, but the second time the weld broke on a steel bar which was designed to hold the block of wood upright whilst it was being split. I rang the supplier and was told "that is unusual we have not had that trouble before it must have been a faulty part" . . . . sound familiar! They were willing to repair it, but I would have to pay for the shipping back to Melbourne, about $60. They offered an alternative, they would send me the replacement part and I could fit it. I reluctantly said, "OK". The part arrived a few days later. It took me an hour and a half to take the machine apart and replace the broken steel bar. The very first time I used the new part, guess what, you got it, the weld broke again in the same place. Again I rang the supplier; more surprise; this time I insisted on my money back. They said that they would give me a refund, but I would still have to pay for the freight to get it back to them. As a compromise, they suggested I get a local welder to re-weld the bar and they would pay the cost. I could have gone to Consumer Affairs with a complaint, but this would have involved a number of letters and phone calls and I just could not be bothered, so I agreed. It ended up costing $80 to get the break re-welded, the supplier did reimburse me, and the machine has been working ever since, but I do not think they made much out of that sale, and I have not been back to them for repeat business nor recommended them to friends.

High Cost of Estimating

We have been largely looking at the effect on companies that produce and sell a standard product which does not change much from year to year (e.g. tools, butter, toys, clothing etc). Let us now look at the companies that design and manufacture non-standard, one-off products and those in the service industries. These companies employ a large workforce of designers and estimators who work up quotes for individual jobs to their customers' specifications (e.g. buildings, equipment, maintenance contracts, ships, specialised tooling). They in turn, have many businesses who supply then with various components, which also require estimating. Estimating represents a significant part of the cost of an operation.

Customers send out requests for quotes, to several manufacturers/ service providers. There can only be one successful bidder, for the rest, their cost of preparing the tender will never be recouped. It is not uncommon for a business to have only a 10% tender success rate. On 21 June 2009, the Sun-Herald Newspaper reported that the Civil Contractors' Federation claimed "tendering for a $1 billion project could cost up to $ 15 million. Contractors, who considered they only had a 20% chance of winning, would not even consider bidding. The high cost of estimating is forcing smaller companies to close or sell their business to larger competitors as they cannot afford to tender for work". Estimating is incredibly time-consuming and a huge waste of time and resources for the firm and for the economy overall. It is also a particularly risky business as it is easy (and not uncommon) to miss a vital step or component from a quote which can significantly reduce profit on the job or even result in a loss.

Every estimate, even the most complex such as a bridge or an office block, is prepared the same way. The project is broken down into smaller jobs, which are then divided into sub-jobs and then basic tasks, each with their own time standards for different sizes, thicknesses, grades, etc. The estimator then uses their historical time standards for labour and machines to build up their cost (e.g. 20 minutes to do a certain size weld, 5 minutes to cut a piece of timber, 8 hours of forklift machine time, 10 hours of labour to paint a certain size room). Next they add a material cost for the items needed for the job, which they may have in stock, or they send out requests to material suppliers for a quote. They then add an amount per hour to cover the company's overheads (like rent, electricity, depreciation of equipment, administration etc.). Finally, a profit mark-up is added to come up with a total price.

Some firms will cut corners or use cheaper materials to reduce their price, which leads to quality and warranty problems. Some firms will cut their standard times and profit margins to win a job which not only puts their long-term viability at risk, but can also send their competitors to the wall. This is contrary to good management practices, and is usually done out of desperation.

As you can see estimating is a complex, expensive and high-risk process. Good estimating is essential to the long-term success and survival of these types of businesses. Would not it be lovely to be able to reduce the risk and cost by 90%?

PROTECTIONISM

At the start of the FES, all countries developed their own industries independently. Freight was very expensive and slow, so international trade was decidedly limited. However during the 20th Century things changed rapidly, global trade became commonplace and this put established industries at risk.

This imbalance eventually led to all Developed Countries introducing regulations to protect local companies against competition from overseas. It involved a number of measures intended to restrict the level of imports; embargoes, which prevented certain products from being imported; annual limits or quotas, on the quantities of some types of imported goods; tariffs, which are an extra cost which has to be paid by importers and subsidies by governments, to local companies to reduce their production costs.

By the 1970's, Protectionism had become extremely expensive for governments to maintain, and international pressure was building for a more liberal trade policy to enable international trading partners more access to local markets. The general feeling amongst politicians was that companies were relying too much on protection and this was stifling any incentive to improve their efficiency. It was also seen that this policy was holding back the progress of Developing Countries; this was considered unfair to them, and ultimately to the detriment of all countries.

By the 1980s, most Developed Countries had agreed to start implementing policies aimed at completely freeing-up international trade (Globalisation). The governments realised that it would be economic and political suicide to try to do this overnight, so they developed plans to allow this to happen on a progressive basis. Their aim was to fully remove trade barriers, except for restrictions on those products that were prohibited due to security concerns and those that were at risk of spreading plant or animal disease. They hoped this would lead to local companies becoming more efficient which would result in lower prices for consumers and greater opportunity for Developing Countries. It was realised that this would be an extremely difficult period of adjustment for many local industries and be very unpopular, but nevertheless at the time it was seen as the right move. The leaders thought that if they introduced this gradually it would give local companies time to become more efficient and competitive, and most would survive; this did not turn out to be the case (see chapter on Globalisation).

In Australia, from 1983, these policies resulted in dramatic increases in the quantity of imported goods in our stores. Today, seven million containers of imported goods arrive by ship each year; everything from clothing, footwear, toys, electronic equipment, whitegoods, furniture, general household consumables, and hardware. The quantity of these goods made in Developing Countries such as China, Thailand, Singapore, Korea, India, Fiji and Poland vastly outnumber those imported from the Developed Countries.

It took a while for governments in Developed Countries to change their minds. They found that some form of protection of local industries needed to be maintained. Today, 30 years further on, all countries (including some Developing Countries) still have or have re-introduced high levels of protection for certain industries, although it is not possible to know the full extent. Governments can be very discrete (some would say underhanded) in their dealings. There are many less obvious, indirect forms of assistance provided, like favouring (at extra cost) local companies in awarding Government contracts, providing research incentives, and grants, subsidising costs like power and training, and tax-free periods for new companies.

For example, in Australia, it was reported in 2004 (The Herald April 30) that sugar farmers were to receive $444 million as a federal industry rescue package. The reason given for this was the failure of a free trade deal with the United States which the growers had been counting on. World sugar prices were at a record low of 0.3 US cents per kilo. Part of the deal was payments to some growers to leave the industry.

In 2009, the trade unions were pushing for the Government to introduce a 20% price subsidy in tenders for government purchasing contracts. An Essential Research poll showed that 85% of Australians agreed that when the Government was buying goods and services they "should buy Australian-made even of it costs a little more" (The Sun-Herald 26th July 2009).

This was opposed by the Government at the time, but then in February 2013 they announced a $1 billion package to assist local industries to win contracts and retain jobs in our country. Do they really know what they are doing or just shooting from the hip?

According to The Australian newspaper (6th June 2012) the government is spending $9.8 billion a year on industry protection. The assistance is mainly being given to the car, clothing, and agricultural industries.

A Protectionist policy did initially save companies and jobs, but it stifled efficiency. Its removal has led to even greater problems. We need to come up with a system which will achieve its aims without the detrimental effects.

THE SHORTCOMINGS OF GLOBALISATION

The aims of Globalisation are:

- To increase the living standards in the underdeveloped countries of the World. This, it is hoped, will have the noble consequence of improving health in the poorer countries, reduce poverty, and maybe even relieve resentment and reduce political tensions.

- To promote Capitalism by increasing competition, and thus increase the efficiency of companies and reduce prices. The theory is that each nation will produce goods for which they have a natural advantage (i.e. the cheapest cost of production), and this will benefit everyone in the World . . . . eventually.

At the start of Globalisation in the 1980s, there was a definite improvement in the efficiency of industries in Australia. Many companies had become fat and lazy under the protection of import quotas and tariffs; they now had to battle to stay competitive. At first Developed Countries became more productive as they slowly increased their skill base, modernised their machinery and responded to pressure to keep wages under control. It soon became obvious, however, that the improvement required for them to be competitive in an open international market, was not achievable, they just could not compete with those countries whose labour costs are one tenth of theirs.

Since the 1980s, competition from Developing Countries has forced an ever increasing number of companies in Developed Countries to either close, relocate their manufacturing facilities overseas to countries like Taiwan, Indonesia, Thailand, Korea, Malaysia and more recently China and India or to replace a lot of their local materials and components with those from Developing Countries.

What happens to a company's employees if it is forced to downsize or close due to Globalisation? To avoid mass unemployment, the Developed Countries are faced with a huge expense in retraining their redundant labour force to work in other markets where they still have a natural advantage. If this trend continues, there will eventually not be enough "other" industries to absorb these unfortunate workers. This is leading to higher unemployment and inevitably to economic decline. Developed Countries will have to reduce their costs by reducing wage rates and their standards of living to a much lower level than they currently enjoy—they are not about to let that happen! I feel that left unchecked, these negative forces have the power to bring down a political party, and maybe even push a country to the brink of war, if people feel their lifestyle is being threatened.

A prime example of the decline to which I refer can be readily seen in our country areas. Where a modest farm was once able to provide a good living for several families it is now lucky to be able to support a farmer's immediate family; our farmers are now among our lowest income earners in the country. The population of many country towns has been declining for the last 25 years.

The other sector that has been particularly hard hit is manufacturing. I started work in 1968 with a large national company in the steel industry in Newcastle, Australia. Like many cities in Developed Countries at that time, it was based around heavy industry. The steel industry and associated businesses employed about 50,000 people, which was about 1/3 of the region's workforce. The location was ideally suited for this industry; it was a major shipping port, next to the coal fields and close to its largest market, Sydney, the largest city in Australia.

51

The industry was protected from overseas competition by tariffs, and all these companies thrived until the 1980s when the tariffs were gradually removed by the Australian Government. There was a rapid decline in sales, which resulted in all leading steel manufacturing businesses in the town closing over the next 20 years. This is a common story for most traditional manufacturing in Developed Countries.

In August 2011 the management of Australia's largest steel manufacturer, BlueScope Steel, announced "it was on the edge of disaster". They told their employees that they had to halve their steel output and shed 1,000 workers. There were also 400 contract workers and suppliers who were badly affected by these cuts.

Globalisation, up to now, has adversely affected the Primary (agriculture) and Secondary (manufacturing) Industries of the Developed Countries, but we are also starting to see a similar decline in the associated Tertiary Industries such as insurance, airline, restaurant, hotel, freight, and retail. Even many professions in "Western" countries that were considered "safe" like Information Technology, Engineering, Design, Telecommunications, and Investment Banking are now under threat as these services are progressively being taken over by countries like India, China, Singapore, and Malaysia. Who would have ever thought we would see the day when companies like General Motors, Chrysler, Toyota, and Sony would be struggling to compete and survive.

In order for a company to prosper it needs to replace its equipment as it wears out, this also gives it the opportunity to take advantage of technological improvements and upgrade to a more productive asset. Companies should be putting money aside for this program, so that when the time comes they have the funds available, but few do, preferring to borrow the money when the time comes. Over the last 30 years, for many companies in Developed Countries, faced with increased competition from overseas, this has not been possible. As a result, they have been working on borrowed time; they have delayed the inevitable failure of their business by running their aged equipment into the ground. This has spread the impact of Globalisation over a longer period and disguised its severity.

Of course, there are some long-established international companies from Developed Countries that have been making quality goods and good profits and continue to do so, these are largely servicing the upper end of the market, but even these companies are starting to find it is getting mighty crowded at the top, and margins are dropping.

As world trade depends on the healthy consumption of goods by the Developed Countries I cannot see Globalisation ever achieving its aims. The reduction in incomes in these countries will lead to **all** countries being worse off. We are living at artificially high standards of living propped up by high levels of borrowing and debt—this cannot continue.

The Global Financial Crises of 2008 has brought this issue to a head as we can see with the current European Crises and the financial problems being experienced in the United States and Japan. Voters in Developed Countries will strongly resist a decrease in their living standards. They will try to force their

Governments to abandon this policy and return to a more protectionist-style of economy. We can already see these forces in action at the distressing protests at the International G8 and G20 Conferences; global protests against austerity measures and the high unemployment caused by the current crisis.

When Globalisation started in Australia in the early 1980's most people were terribly concerned about their future, but the politicians said not to worry, it would all work itself out, job losses in one sector would be absorbed by other growing industries like mining, professional services, emerging "smart industries", and tourism. Do we really want to be dependent on tourism and mining? Tourism smells to me like a master/servant relationship and mining is at the bottom of the value-adding process. With our high level of education and skilled workforce we should be aiming to make high quality goods. The Government's support of efforts to build "smart industries" has been half-hearted, and many companies have had to take their inventions overseas to have them financed.

The problem is not just that Developing Countries have lower costs, but also that some unscrupulous companies in these countries engage in "dumping" which is the selling a product at less than its overseas costs to build up market share. This practice seriously damages the local industry in the Developed Countries, and can lead to an industry's demise if allowed to continue. A prime example was in 2009 (The Sun-Herald Newspaper 7th February 2010) when the Australian Customs Department reported the dumping of toilet paper (a particularly appropriate example do not you think) by the Asia Pulp and Paper company. They said tens of millions of rolls were dumped on the Australian market, undercutting the local product by up to 40%. This resulted in a ban on this product. Most of this paper came from mills in China and Indonesia. In Indonesia, the company was accused of logging in rainforests used by endangered orang-utans.

Another problem, which is on the increase, is the counterfeiting of goods, that is the importing and selling of cheap fakes of many famous brands. Many items of clothing, shoes, jewellery, bags, and watches are being targeted by these crooks. This is really hurting these popular brands and will result in their destruction if it is allowed to continue.

Globalisation has been sold to the public as saving us money by making companies more efficient. Individual companies may have reduced their costs, but what would we see if we could calculate the effect on the whole of the country's economy? If we were to include all hidden costs like lost leave entitlements; retraining of the workforce; bankruptcies; unpaid debts to suppliers and contractors; unemployment benefits; extra cost to the health and law enforcement services and government (taxpayers) funding to prop up failing industries (like the motor, steel and sugar industry), we would soon see that the system is a sham, and needs to be exposed and changed.

In 2012, one of Australia's largest construction companies collapsed financially with $17 million owing to 600 creditors. Another building company, Holmwood builders (trading as Procorp) also collapsed owing $ 8 million to 500 creditors. These are just a couple of examples of many construction companies which have failed over the last few years with the same sad stories of bad debts.

In 2002, Hunt Corporation in Philadelphia decided to outsource manufacturing of its office and graphics supplies, to contractors in China. They were established in 1899, and have 900 employees. They used to despatch their goods in days or at worst weeks, but with outsourcing this blew out to an average of 95 days. This increase in their lead times caused their inventory and overnight shipping charges also to rise. How would this have affected their sales and are they better off?

I think most politicians who at the time, supported this policy, genuinely thought it would work. If they could have envisaged the massive economic upheaval and the destruction of many of their key industries, I am sure they would have never have agreed to follow such a dangerous strategy. Are we really doing the underdeveloped and developing countries any favours with our present model? Would not it be marvellous if we could come up with a system that would achieve the original goals of Globalisation without the pain?

ELIMINATING EXPLOITATION

In Developed Countries, it used to be the case that hard work was rewarded with a good income. Whatever happened to "a fair day's work for a fair day's pay". Many small-to-medium business owners work very long hours to run and build their businesses. As we have discussed in other chapters, these businesses are often high-risk ventures that more often than not fail. Is this a case of exploitation by consumers? As a community, we should be rewarding enterprise and protecting these businesses from risk after all they are the principal employers in our country. According to the Australian Bureau of Statistics, "small business (less than 20 employees for non-manufacturing and fewer than 100 for manufacturing) accounts for 96% of all businesses and 50% of employment in this country. Large national conglomerates are forcing down the price of goods and services, is not this exploitation of our farmers, fishermen, truck drivers and small producers!

In America, the heart of Capitalism, it is harder than ever for people in low socioeconomic groups to build a business empire.

The prohibitive cost of getting a college degree, the low incomes paid to the majority of workers, the high tax paid by the lower classes compared with the rich, and the practice of "jobs for the boys" where the good jobs are given to family, and friends of the upper-classes, means 90% of the population never gets any chance to become rich. The share of US Gross National Product (Income) earned by lower class workers was increasing during the 19th, and early part of the 20th Centuries, but has dropped significantly since the 1960s. According to Harver Analytics, Gluskin Sheff (see graph below) the percentage declined from 67.5 in 1960 to 57.5 in 2010—a 15% drop, and the most disturbing thing is there is a sharp future trend in the downward direction.

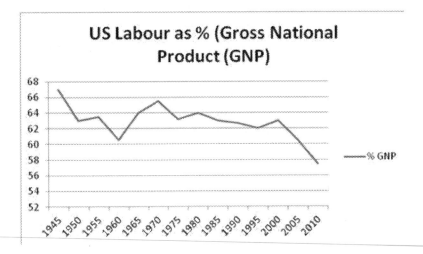

In Developing Countries exploitation is blatant; most workers are getting paid below the poverty line, and cannot support their family. Many people are idle as their country's economy is so poor there are no jobs. People are dying in their millions from disease due to unsanitary living conditions and malnutrition.

These countries' land and resources are being pillaged, farmers' land is being taken from them, and the poor in the cities are being kicked out of their modest homes to make way for "progress". Many workers are forced to work in unsafe conditions, in dangerous mines and factories. Globalisation was supposed to improve the living standards in these countries, but this is not the case for the lower classes. In 2009, the US Department of Labour reported (The Herald newspaper Sept 12) that "122 goods were produced with forced labour, child labour or both, in 58 countries from Afghanistan to North Korea to Uzbekistan". Child labour is used to produce cotton, sugar, tobacco, coffee, rice, bricks, carpets, clothing, gold, coal, strawberries, and pornography in various countries like Burma, India, the Philippines, Thailand and Argentina.

The affluent countries donate over $100 Billion per year in international aid to underdeveloped countries. In many countries, the aid is not reaching the poor it is intended to help. One shocking example was reported in 2005 (The Sydney Morning Herald 26 June), the previous rulers of Nigeria had stolen or misused AUD$520 billion (yes billion) over a period of 39 years, up to 1999, when the country returned to civilian rule. This is not an isolated case, but it is impossible to know exactly how much of the aid is siphoned off by corrupt rulers and officials. Just giving money to the poorer countries obviously does not work. I am sure the people of these countries would much prefer to have jobs, and support themselves rather than relying on charity.

In 2009, the UN Food and Agricultural Agency said that 1 billion people in the World do not have enough to eat, and that this was a historic high. It was not just the population of the poorer nations that were starving—they said that it includes 15 million people from Developed Countries.

International companies are setting up subsidiary branches in underdeveloped countries to extract that country's valuable resources. Some of these companies then, through a process called "transfer pricing", sell the subsidiary's produce to the parent company in their home country at a price which is much below its true value on the global market, thereby reducing the subsidiary's profit. This is deliberately designed to avoid paying tax in the source country. Why does the international community allow this to happen? These companies should be forced to pay the poorer countries a fair price for their labour and resources, and a fair rate of company tax, rather than giving them charity.

"The rich get richer, and the poor . . . . get the scraps". Exploitation at any level will breed contempt which eventually turns into hatred which will ultimately turn-around (it might take 20 years), and bite you.

ENVIRONMENT

The Industrial Revolution led to a rapid rise in living standards in western nations. While this is good for the people, it has been bad for the planet. High living standards mean a greater consumption of goods and hence more waste. There has been a rapid decline in the quality of our environment caused by an ever-increasing demand for resources, associated industrial pollution, and an explosion in the World's population. Ancient forests are disappearing at an exponential rate, pristine rivers are being polluted, farmland is being degraded, and our air and drinking water contaminated by our waste. Less than 50% of the original forests remain—most of this destruction has occurred in the last 50 years. This has led to a tragic loss of habitat for native animals and indigenous plants. We are experiencing an alarming rate of species extinction with many more on the brink, species are being annihilated at a rate more than 100 times faster than would happen naturally (i.e. without human interference) through evolution. It is estimated that the historical average life-span of a species has been about 10 million years. **Some scientists predict that 50% of the species alive today could be extinct by 2100, and that the speed at which they are being**

lost is faster today than any other time in history. Now these are frightening thoughts—what are YOU doing about it?

In 2002, I saw an advertisement in one of our junk-mail brochures for a ream (500 pages) of A4 paper for $4.00. I was astounded, in the 1980s I recall paying $10.00 per ream yet here we were some 15 years later, and the price had fallen 60% or 80% if you take inflation into account. During this period, there had been numerous reports in the news about the destruction of the World's endangered old-growth forests for timber and the out-of-control clearing of forests in many countries (including Australia), for farmland and housing—how can the price have dropped so much? In theory, you would have expected the forces of supply and demand to have caused the price to have quadrupled in this time. At $4.00, there is little incentive for people to be frugal in their use of paper for photocopying and printing. If the price was $40.00 it would certainly make people and companies think twice about how much they were using, and how to reduce their consumption. This product was one of the main reasons I decided to try and do something about the state of the World and our future. What has happened to the price in the 11 years since 2002? . . . . it has now fallen even further to below $4.00!

It is getting harder for people to make a living from the land. Our World is becoming less productive each year as we use up and erode our rich top-soils which have taken many thousands of years to form. Our farmlands have been badly contaminated by chemicals, acid rain, and salinity. In addition to these powerful corporations are putting more pressure on the farmers to reduce their price, this can only be achieved by cutting costs which is often at the expense of long-term sustainable practices (e.g. resting paddocks, removal of weeds, planting trees in strategic locations, developing water-saving practices, controlling pests, preventing erosion and salinity), and using more chemicals, which will have a long-term, detrimental effect on our ecosystems. What reasonable person would destroy the very environment on which they and their family rely for their sustenance and indeed their very survival? We need to give farmers a fair price for their produce, so they can use environmentally-friendly practices whilst still earning a good return on their investment.

Scientists say that the vast majority of the Earth's species are still unknown. From what I can see, estimates of the number of species vary from 2 million to 100 million; extinction rates are estimated to be between 10,000 and 100,000 per year—but nobody actually knows. They say that only 1.75 million have been described so far. What we do know is that the World's ecology is extremely complicated; we do not fully understand the benefits we get from an individual species let alone from 13 million. Apart from our general moral responsibility to preserve life, we need to minimise the damage we are doing to our planet's biodiversity, as we are sure to be annihilating many species, which are critical to our own long-term survival.

Most Developed Countries have started to take action to make their production and living practices more sustainable, but change is exceedingly slow. Unfortunately, the message has still to get through to many of the Developing Countries who still show a poor regard for the environment.

About ten years ago scientists started warning us that our planet's Geosphere was being stressed by "Global Warming". This is the rising in the temperature of the Earth's atmosphere primarily caused by increasing concentrations of greenhouse gases produced by human activities such as the burning of fossil fuels and deforestation. The temperature had been rising for some time, but particularly since the 1980s. They warned that, based on current trends, it will rise by several more degrees during the 21st Century, unless immediate and drastic action is taken. At that time, the evidence was statistical—temperature charts, measurements of the ozone layer, and recording glacial melts, which did not really ring alarm bells with most people.

It is only just now, when it is starting to impact on our daily lives (and cost us money) that this issue is getting our attention. Global Warming is obviously a dreadful thing, but if it can jolt people and governments into remedial action then it may herald the start of serious worldwide cooperation. Maybe now that we are experiencing record: summer heat, winter snowfalls, floods, bush fires, storms, sea surges, mud slides, and ice-cap melts that the World will take notice and make the changes necessary to avoid the pending catastrophe.

Three million years ago our ancestors were smart enough to stand upright and start using tools. We have gotten smarter, but not wiser. Our species should, on average, last another seven million years—let this not be the century that ends it.

Waste of the World's Limited Resources

The World's non-renewable resources like topsoil, coal, iron ore, copper, nickel, natural gas, oil etc are limited. We are using them up at a rate unprecedented in history; is this fair to our children and future generations?

For power, we rely mainly on coal and oil; everyone accepts we are running out rapidly. There is a common belief that science will manage to come up with some brilliant new development which will replace these resources before they are completely gone, and maybe this is right, but should not we give the scientists as much time as possible to do their work? **Slowing down the rate at which we use up these resources should be one of our foremost objectives and priorities.**

The increased usage of coal has been particularly driven home to me in a highly personal way. I live in Newcastle which is the largest coal exporting port in the World. It has been alarming over the years to see the rapid growth of this business; it is not uncommon to have over 50 gigantic bulk carriers off our shore, awaiting loading. There are huge scars on our Valley's landscape, problems with coal dust and weekly conflict with other landowners. Nobody is disputing the need for coal, but it is the speed of growth in demand that is causing concern.

At present, the main contenders for replacing coal and oil are nuclear energy and coal seam gas, but both of these have side-effects which are seen by many people to be too dangerous for mankind and the environment. In the case of nuclear energy, in its 60 year history there have been many accidents (search Wikipedia for a list) and several major disasters (Three Mile Islands, Chernobyl, Sellafield, and Fukushima). Several Russian submarines have been sunk which pose a threat of radioactive pollution of our oceans. I am sure there have been many smaller incidences that we never hear about where nuclear power is used for civilian and defence purposes. Considering Plutonium-239 has a half-life of 24,000 years, in my opinion it is far too risky to chance. Nuclear currently only accounts for a small percentage of the World's power, imagine what could happen if it ever got to 50% or more.

In the case of coal seam gas, scientists see this as a cheap source of fuel, but there are serious problems in regards to the safety of its method of extraction; will methane escape into the atmosphere and increase the rate of global warming; will it affect the artesian water tables; will it affect the rivers? These are questions which will take time to answer; we need to be sure of the consequences before we start using this technique.

Most companies deliberately build obsolescence into their products, the quicker something wears out, the sooner it will be replaced, but this policy has a devastating effect on our environment. Many of the products we use contain toxic chemicals, gases or metals, most of which end up in landfill, so it makes even more sense to limit the use of these materials whenever possible.

In Developed Countries manufacturing has become extremely capital intensive (i.e. machines are replacing people), and workers are being paid more which has increased their living standards. This means goods are cheaper to manufacture, but more expensive to repair as it requires the use of manual labour. For example, take a bicycle, you have to pay AUD$1,500 for anything reasonable, and AUD$5,000 for a top range bike. At department stores you can buy a new bike (made in Asia) for under AUD$100. It would cost this much to replace the cogs and chain when they wear out, so what do consumers do? Of course, they buy a new one, and their old one goes to the dump after only a couple of years. The cheap bikes look terrific and appear to have all of the features of the expensive ones, but of course they are poor quality, and parts quickly wear out, bend or break.

We need to make better products that last longer, this would result in things being more expensive to buy initially, but they would be more reliable, be more enjoyable to use, give better service, and people would choose to get them repaired rather than replacing them. Contrary to what a lot of people think, I have found that longer-term, buying quality actually saves me money.

Another example—I needed to replace my old mattress last month. The new queen-sized ones I looked at ranged in price from $400 to $6,000. I chose a reasonable quality one, worth $2,300 (on "sale"). I know it will last for at least 15 years, and will pleasure me with blissful sleep, 8 hours per night, for 5,475 nights in that time. Now I could have bought the cheapest one, but what would I have gotten—after a couple of years; a lumpy bed with squeaky springs, interrupted sleep, and a bad back, that is what! I would have undoubtedly got fed-up, and have had to replace it after 5 or 6 years, I would have saved a few dollars, but at what cost to my comfort and health. The most frustrating thing to me is that the amount of material used to make the cheapest one would be the same as the dearest, therefore I would have contributed to three times the land-fill.

When we got married we bought a top-of-the-range Sunbeam toaster, it was made to last with stainless steel, which was expensive at the time. It was one of the first "automatic" models which lowered and raised the toast gently and sensed when it was cooked (as opposed to simple timing mechanisms)—perfectly every time. One of the elements broke after 15 years. We had been so happy with its performance we were keen to get it repaired rather than buying a new one. It broke down twice more over the next 15 years and each time we made the same decision, get it repaired. Finally, the parts were no longer available, so it had to be replaced. We bought a new, reputable brand toaster, but it was terribly slow, and cooked the toast unevenly on each side. We had to take the bread out when it was half cooked, and turn it around. After 2 years of perseverance we gave up on this model, and bought a different brand, it was faster, but still did not cook as evenly as our old Sunbeam. This was 2 years ago—it will be interesting to see how long it lasts!

The rate of technological change is another threat to our resources. Early televisions were expensive, but they used to last for 10 years plus. Our first computer and electronic games machines lasted 6-8 years—technology was moving slowly. Then things started to heat up, changes started coming more frequently. Manufacturers realised that if they had more frequent releases of the software, screens and computer chips, and did a good job of marketing the new features then they could grow their businesses faster and make more money. They set about persuading consumers that the latest models were essential to maximising enjoyment and productivity with the aim of getting them to upgrade before the old model was worn out. This is resulting in many electronic items, which still worked fine, being discarded. As more manufacturers entered the market, prices dropped, and so too did margins. Companies had to find more creative ways to increase the quantities they sold. This has resulted in new models and operating systems being released every year, often without being thoroughly tested and debugged (they say that Microsoft's programs have hundreds of thousands of bugs). In the last 2 months, two of my friends have reported buying new LCD televisions and having problems with their screens. Setting a more realistic price and quality (including bug-free software) for electronic items, and removing the threat of price-wars would encourage companies to slow down the pace of change, and spend more time developing and testing, before releasing new versions. A higher price would also dissuade consumers from changing models as often.

My city has a twice-yearly collection of the larger household rubbish which cannot fit into our weekly garbage bin. Every time the streets are littered with enormous amounts of rubbish awaiting collection—TVs, fridges, lawn mowers, beds, chairs, garden furniture, CD players, computers, tools, clothes, toys etc. You can tell many of these items are less than 5 years old. Prior to the 1960s, these items would have given double the period of service they do now; lounges used to last for 50 years, it was not uncommon to see fridges which were 20 years old, clothes held together and were often thread-bare before being discarded into the cleaning rag box, and toys were passed from sons and daughters to grandchildren. The reason for this was partly due to the fact that our parents valued their possessions and repaired broken parts, but also because items were built to last. Lounges were bolted, screwed and glued not just stapled together, springs were made out of good quality steel, fridges were solid, tables, and cabinets had dove-tailed joints, toys were held together with dowelling and glue and bicycles were made to take a long, hard life.

In the building industry, there is no way half the houses built today will be around in 80 years time, let alone in 200 years. Many commercial buildings are demolished after only 50 years as the cost of maintaining them is greater than the cost of replacing. How much extra would it cost to double the life of our buildings, 30%, 50%; it makes financial sense to do so, and it would contribute to preserving the World's limited resources?

The use of plastic started to become common in the 1970s. Over the next 30 years it became the ubiquitous product, it was everywhere, and used for everything from wrapping paper to cars. When I was young milk was sold in glass bottles, empties were collected, washed and reused. Plastic became a cheaper alternative for companies. These days it is all sold in plastic milk bottles. Until recently these went straight into land fill, but now people are encouraged to re-cycle, so this has at least reduced the problem. Over the last 10 years, there has also been a growing resistance to the use of plastic bags—billions of plastic bags were being thrown into our waste every year. At least now they are being made more biodegradable; stores are starting to once again use paper bags, and consumers are encouraged to bring their own cloth shopping bags. Call me old-fashion, but I would still like to see drinks in bottles again.

We need to change our mindset. Mankind seems to feel that the Earth has an infinite capacity to sustain and an infinite capacity to dispose of waste—this is rubbish (excuse the pun)! Like all other successful species on this planet we need to learn to live in harmony with others, and within the planets ability to support us. If you draw a time-line 1 kilometre long to represent the history of life on Earth, the last part, less than the width of a human hair, would represent mankind's existence. Yet we have used up more resources and damaged the planet more than any other species. How are the Earth's limited resources going to last for the next 1,000 years let alone the next 500,000 years at this level of extravagance?

Now we all know what is happening, no excuses, we are bombarded with these facts every week, but what are we doing about it—very little it seems. It is time to stop burying our heads in the sand and take a stand. Let's say "stop, we are going to change direction, and we are going to do it NOW". This must be a clear policy by all nations. I believe we can make changes that will substantially reduce the use of our limited resources and extend the life of our reserves—this is a crucial part of the solution I am proposing.

Abuse of Transportation

Up to 60 years ago goods were generally consumed near where they were grown or made. The exception to this was where items were produced which were unique to a particular area, due to its climatic or geographic location (e.g. minerals, spices, wool, oil). With improvements to and the reduction in the cost of transportation, it has become common for goods to be sent and sold to any part of the Globe; clothing from Asia; oranges from South America; matches from the South Pacific etc. Freighting goods around the country and the World uses vast quantities of oil and other fuels. Large quantities of minerals are required to manufacture the millions of trucks and thousands of ships and planes require for this trade. Surely we can find a better use for these resources than the unnecessary shunting of goods from one part of the World to another.

All these products were, and can be, easily made again by the Western Countries. When I was a boy, I lived in a mid-sized city, in New South Wales. There were vegetable gardens, dairy farms, a meat abattoir, and fruit orchards on the outskirts of town which supplied the needs of the local markets—these have now disappeared. Last week at breakfast I checked the labels on my food: I had milk from Queensland (1200kms away), butter from Western Australia (6000km away), and jam from Victoria (1000km away) . . . . at least the bread was local . . . . for now!

When companies consider their cost of transport they do not take into account the true cost. In Australia, trucks pay an annual registration fee and tax on the fuel they use, but this falls far short of the cost of building and maintaining roads and bridges which they use and damage, the taxpayer ends up subsidising the rest. "One legal 80,000 pound GVW (30 tonne) tractor-trailer truck does as much damage to road pavement as 9,600 cars". (US Highway Research Board, NAS, 1962)—they certainly do not contribute 9,600 times the revenue in fees and taxes. Research has also shown that based on the kilometres travelled, trucks are more likely to be involved in serious accidents than cars, and when a truck is involved there is a high chance someone will die. When we look at the costs of transport we should take into account, the cost of these accidents; the cost of the police, rescue services, health services, and legal fees. With shipping, we should be taking into account the cost of the pollution of our seas by oil leaks and accidents. According to NewScientist magazine there are 10,000 containers lost at sea each year. In 2011, the London Telegraph reported that in 2009 37 bulk carriers sank—what kind of a time-bomb are we creating, what will be the cost to clean up this mess in the future.

Taking these hidden costs into account is it really cheaper to buy an item from another country or another part of our country— we would not have a clue of the true cost, but you do not have to be an accountant, let's just apply a bit of common sense—how can it possibly be cheaper to get a carton of milk from a dairy 1,200 kilometres away or oranges from South America! Let us get back to supporting local producers.

Population Control

We now have the history and knowledge to realise what damage continual population growth is doing to our planet, to our lifestyles, and indeed to our very survival. Science has now given us the means to control it, all we now need is the commitment.

According to the World Bank our planet currently has 7 billion people, and this is set to increase to 10 billion within 40 years. Our planet's ability to support human beings is finite, nobody knows the absolute limit. Science is continually extending this limit through more productive ways to grow food (e.g. green houses, aquaculture, fertilisers, cross-breeding) and enhancing nature (e.g. desalination plants, genetic engineering, insect control), but I feel our population is far exceeding the speed at which science is meeting the challenge.

Feeding the people is one thing, disposing of waste is another! What irreversible damage is all this burning, burying, and dumping doing to our land, air and water? Make no mistake; there will be a time of reckoning, and the lager the population, the sooner it will come.

Why do we need to keep finding smarter ways to cope with this problem, this is not getting to the root of the problem. If we just kept the population at a sustainable level, then we would not need worry about how we were going to feed an extra 3 billion people in 40 years time.

Most Developed Countries have reached the point of a stable population through natural growth; some are even reducing their numbers. Their total population may be increasing, but this is due to immigration or taking in refugees, escaping from their homeland. The growth in the World's population is occurring in the Developing Countries. I feel overcoming poverty and increasing the standard of living, health and education in these poorer nations, would lead to a reduction in the birth rate, as it has in the affluent nations. The sooner and faster we can do this the better. Enough said!

WORLD PEACE

Once you start thinking about a solution to the problems of Globalisation you soon realise the inter-relationship to other social issues. Repression and exploitation have been the catalyst for many revolutions. Improvements in an underdeveloped country's standard of living, giving its people meaningful work and helping them feel that they are playing an important part on the world stage must have a considerable effect on its peoples' happiness and self-esteem. I believe that this, more than anything, would contribute to eventually achieving World Peace. This would not happen quickly as there is still a lot of ingrained anger and hatred which would need to subside, and this may take a few generations. To achieve World Peace people have to work together, they have to be concerned about their fellow man; they must have mutual respect and treat them as equals. People need to have a stable job which gives them sufficient money to meet their primary needs and feel safe. One thing I know for sure is that it will not happen by accident, if we ever hope to achieve a better life for all the peoples of the World then we need a universal system and the visionary leaders to make it happen. I believe we can achieve this without damaging any of our current standards of living, whilst still maintaining the cultures and religions of all people.

Between 2001 and 2005, we saw three of the worst examples yet of the horror of international terrorism with the attacks on the World Trade Centre in the United States, and the bombings in Bali and London, but what is actually behind these attacks? At first it appears that religious hatred and differences in ideology are behind terrorism, but I think this is just the manifestation of the root cause, which is the resentment and envy between the rich and poor. The lesser-developed countries see the lifestyles and excesses of the Western Nations, particularly the USA, and they feel that much of what these countries have today has been achieved by exploiting the less, well-off countries, and they have good reason to think so.

I am not blaming the current Developed Nations because this has been going on for at least 5,000 years. Exploitation over the millenniums, by the Anglo Saxons, the Vikings, the Persians, the Romans, the Chinese, the Mayans, the Incas, the British, the Spanish, the French, the Germans, and others has created a world of fear, hatred and suspicion. Even in these times when the World is supposed to be at peace; millions of people are being killed every year in civil and neighbourhood wars . . . . and we call ourselves "civilized"!

How much does war and the arms race cost the Developed Countries? Reducing international tensions and internal civil wars will free up funds for more humanitarian purposes. Brown University in the US estimates the recent and current wars in

Iraq, Afghanistan and Pakistan will cost 3 to 4 trillion dollars and resulted in the death of 250,000 people.

A trading system that builds peoples' dignity and creates a reasonable standard of living for all people will go a long way towards healing old wounds not just between countries, but also between social classes within a country. I believe reducing the differential between the rich and poor will promote the spread of peace throughout the World. Capitalism will still be a prime element of such a system; some will always have more than others (this is healthy as it provides motivation to improve oneself), but the wealth needs to be more fairly shared.

"You may say I'm a dreamer, but I'm not the only one.
I hope someday you will join us, and the World will live as one"
—John Lennon, 'Imagine' 1975

SOLUTION

The eminent British economist, Alfred Marshall, deduced that it was human behaviour that leads to better living standards. He spent his lifetime studying businesses. His conclusion was, that it was the sum of individual endeavour to produce more output, with fewer resources (material and labour), that was causing productivity and efficiency to increase, and this was primarily responsible for raising living standards. Thousands of new ideas and a continuous push for improvement, accumulated across the nation were increasing wages and wealth. I agree with him—which I am sure he would be very pleased to know if he was still alive! If he is right, then in order to increase the living standards in the underdeveloped countries, we need a system which will give them an incentive to be innovative, and strive for better methods and improved products. Is our current system doing this; I think not. FES and Globalisation, as they work now, are degrading the quality of goods in all countries. In Developed Countries they are causing an upheaval of the workforce which is destroying the incentive of workers to work harder to better themselves, and stifling investment and innovation.

Wouldn't it be great to find a way for Developed Countries to maintain their standard of living while at the same time assisting Developing Countries to quickly increase theirs? This is a very complex matter, but I believe this goal is achievable, however, it would require a much greater level of co-operation between countries, than we have at present. The change would need to be made by governments, but the initiative would have to come from the majority of the population, the workers, and small business owners for it is they, who have the most to gain. We used to have a situation where all the wealth and power was in the hands of Western Nations, but this will not be the case in the future. We need to work out a way to handle this transition, so it will be to the benefit of all without destroying existing economies.

What follows is my outline for such change, which I feel, is achievable. I have called it "The Fair Dinkum Economy". What does "Fair Dinkum" mean? In Australia, it is used to describe something or someone that is "genuine, honest, admirable and true". I thought it was the ideal term to describe an economic model for future trade relationships between countries which is fair to all parties and benefits all parties. Surely what every compassionate person eventually would like to see, is all countries living in harmony, with a reasonable living standard.

There have been 3 substantial developments over the last 50 years that have given us the means to achieve this

These developments are:

- Technological developments—the invention of electronic data processing and the development of the Internet has given us cheap and fast communications, available to anyone, anywhere. This, coupled with the improvements to telecommunications, has the potential to give everyone ready access to information, so they can see what is happening in the rest of the World. It allows people of all languages to communicate with each other, and has given the masses a universal voice.

- The development of sophisticated software to enable the rapid estimating of costs. Some of these international packages are multilingual and feature automatic foreign currency conversions.

- The invention of cheap and effective chemical contraception. Families can now plan the number of children they will have.

How do we harness these new opportunities to create a better world?

Aims of The Fair Dinkum Economy

When you travel the World you realise how warm and friendly the common people are, it doesn't matter whether they are from the deserts, the tropics or the polar regions, the thing that strikes me is that they all have the same loves and desires. Before you start on a journey, you firstly need to understand where you want to go, so I firstly had to work out what it was I was trying to achieve, how would I know if the changes I am proposing are successful? Once I established those goals I then worked backwards, identifying and analysing the current problems, and trying to come up with ways to overcome them. I wanted to be driven primarily by peoples' basic needs, but I also had to keep in mind the needs of our planet, after all if our Biosphere does not survive then neither will the people.

So what are peoples' basic needs, and are they common to all races? The Dalai Lama maintains that the strongest desire of all people is for happiness. Surely nobody in their right mind would want to wake up each morning to a life of death, destruction and hunger. Working on this premise, what do we have to achieve in order to be happy?

My list of aims would be:-

- to live in safety and peace,
- to have suitable shelter and clothing, and be well fed,
- to be respected and loved,
- to feel we are living worthwhile lives.

In regards to our planet, my list would be:-

- for humans to live a sustainable lifestyle,
- to stabilise our population
- to reduce the consumption of non-renewable resources, to make stocks last as long as possible for the sake of future generations.

How do we structure an economic model to achieve these aims? I think it needs to contain the following properties:-

- Increase living standards in ALL countries (not some at the expense of others).
- Maximise the use of the global labour workforce (low unemployment).
- Improve skills in underdeveloped countries.
- Strive for greater efficiency and productivity.
- Improve the quality of goods and services.
- Avoid wasting resources.
- Maintain and improve the environment.
- Reduce friction between countries in World Trade.
- Eliminate population growth as quickly as possible.

International trade is the best and quickest way to raise the living standards of Developing Countries, but in order to do this we need to be able to control the setting of prices to ensure the exporting countries get a reasonable return, and the economies of the importing countries are not damaged in the process.

We need to stop relying on "price" to attract buyers, and replace it with "quality". We need to educate buyers that it is worth paying a premium for quality, a decision based solely on price is usually false economy in the longer-term.

What I propose is the setting of an international minimum market prices for all imported goods, this would be the lowest price that an imported item could be sold at anywhere in the World. The way this price is set is explained in the following chapters, therefore for now, I will use a simple example to explain the way I see this system working.

A hypothetical example—Buying a pair of shoes:

Currently a consumer goes to buy a pair of shoes; they try on two pairs, one made in Australia and the other from China. They like the Australian one, it is more comfortable and wider and has a tough looking sole, but the Chinese one looks almost as nice, and is half the price . . . they buy the Chinese one. They get home and start wearing their new shoes, the inside stitching is rough and at first hurts their feet. They also have a rather unpleasant smell (from the tanning of the leather), but eventually they feel comfortable. At three months, the eyelets start to fall out, at four months the stitching starts to come apart and after six months the sole cracks. The consumer certainly won't buy this brand again, but there are plenty of brands to tempt and confuse them—next time they might try the Polish one or the Indian or maybe another brand from China (probably from the same company without knowing it) . . . . with the same consequences.

What would happen under The Fair Dinkum Economy? The next time the consumer goes to buy shoes, both brands would be the same price. If the both now have the same features and look similar they would invariably buy the Australian shoe as it is a brand they are familiar with and trust. They pay twice the price they did previously, but they get at least 2 years of comfortable wear, so they would better off and happier, as too would the Australian manufacturer and the Australian economy. The Chinese manufacturer would not accept losing their overseas markets. They would fight back; they would source better materials, increase training of their staff, and improve their procedures to improve quality. They would also become more innovative and create better marketing campaigns.

Two years later the same consumer goes to buy their next pair of shoes, but their decision is not so straightforward this time. This time they find that the Chinese and Australian shoes are just as comfortable as each other. The Chinese manufacturer has changed to a softer leather, they have improved the finish on the inside stitching, so it doesn't rub, they have used the same brand of sole as the Australians, and have added some decorative stitching along the seams. The consumer was talking to their mate at the hotel the other night, and he was praising his new Chinese shoes; they decide to give them another go . . . . this time they are very happy with their choice.

It is now up to the Australian manufacturer to get their act together and match or better the competition. This is no different to what they have been doing for decades, but now, finally, they, and the importers are on the same, level playing field.

Some of you may feel this is too much government control, but governments currently have extensive systems, which they use to regulate the way companies in their country can operate. In Developed Countries, there is strict control over safety standards, tax regulations, pollution laws and copious legislation regarding employment. This would be just one more regulation they would have to follow.

This system does not have to be implemented in one hit. I would see it being introduced progressively, one product sector at a time starting with the more stable products (e.g. whitegoods, electrical items and hardware) where it is easier to establish a standard, then working towards introducing the difficult ones (e.g. clothing, food and industrial products), over a period of several years.

The Setting of the Fair International Trade Price (FITP)

The FITP is the minimum price and standard to be set for each item traded between countries.

Each item would be allotted an identity code. This code would be based on a detailed description, including (most importantly), the minimum quality standard to be achieved. There would be a minimum price calculated for the most basic item of a particular style, and this would be the lowest price which can be charged to a customer. It would be set at a level which rewards all people in the supply chain. It would take into account a fair wage for workers, a fair price for material suppliers, a fair profit for the manufacturer (taking into account their investment and risk), and a fair amount to cover the cost and profit of all those involved in the distribution of the goods (importers, wholesalers and freight companies).

By "basic", I mean the lowest level of quality which is required for a particular purpose, to achieve an acceptable result (considering the price paid), for a reasonable period of time. Let me clarify with an example: a watch's price would be based on a certain quality of materials and workmanship which would ensure the watch would keep accurate time, be water resistant, its band would be of a standard which would not rust, flake, break or lose its colour, it would have an alarm, it would be shock-resistant, and have to last for a for a minimum of 15 years. Now there may be more sophisticated models of the same type which have more features (like a stop watch, a light, gold plating etc), and these could be sold for a higher price to justify these added features. All these watches would be one "type", and have the same code. Manufactures of top quality watches (like Seiko and Rolex) would still be able to charge a much higher price for their premium product. There would need to be several other "types" of watches, with different codes, to cover other distinct styles such as a diver's or cyclist's watch; these would also have specific minimum requirements. You may have 1,000 different watch models being imported, all sold at a differing prices, but they would be represented by maybe 5 types, therefore you would only need 5 standard prices and quality standards.

N.B. this standard would not apply to a country's locally produced goods only to imported goods, but I envisage that very soon, consumers would pressure local manufacturers to match this quality standard, if they didn't already.

Let's look at another example, a particular style of camera—a digital compact camera. The team setting the standard and price would establish a list of features that they feel are desirable in this type of camera. This may include features like a flash unit, a 3 times optical zoom, a certain size screen, 10 mega-pixels of memory, and auto focus. It would be required to last for say 10 years. They calculate that a reasonable price is $250 to manufacture and distribute to the market. This camera would then become the cheapest **imported** digital compact camera you could buy in the World; no one would be allowed to sell below this price. International companies would compete to produce the "best" camera at this standard, and this would guarantee consumers a good quality product and good value for money. There would be hundreds of other models manufactured of better quality than this, sold at higher prices as there are now, but there would be no need for more price standards for this type of camera, as free market forces would determine the premiums to be paid for the extra features. All cameras currently manufactured below this minimum standard, which currently range from $10 retail would disappear from the market, and wouldn't this be a good thing. Companies would be allowed to sell off existing stock for a limited period before the changeover to the new system.

When I refer to a "style" for some items this would also cover different sizes, for example, lounge chairs, refrigerators, and electric drills would all have a different FITP for each size.

A system of international labelling would be introduced for all exported goods. RFID microdots would be required to be attached to the product or its packaging, which would show:

- a FITP identification code (consumers would be able to access details on the Internet)
- the description
- the version or model number (this would need to be sequential)
- the date of manufacture
- the country of manufacture
- the manufacture's name

In Australia, as in most countries I expect, in an attempt to save our jobs we try to encourage consumers to buy locally produced goods, where possible. This has proven to be frustratingly difficult. By law, all goods sold in Australia are required to show the country of manufacture, but you will still find many items on stores shelves without this information shown, or where they only show the local importer's name and address. On other items, the manufacturing country is so well hidden that you have to search the whole label to find it . . . . and when you do it is often in minuscule print. Many foodstuffs show "made in Australia from local and imported ingredients" which is pretty useless information. You can fit a lot of data on a microchip; in the case of foodstuffs, which are a mixture of different ingredients, producers would be required to show the identification code of each ingredient in a batch. This would allow consumers to use their smart phones to check the country of origin of each ingredient.

An international body would need to be established, and they would be responsible for setting minimum retail prices for all imported goods and services, based on the average cost of the eight countries with the best standards of living, the "G8" Group (France, Germany, Italy, Japan, United Kingdom, United States, Canada, and Russia). Why the top eight countries? I suggest this, so that current standards of living can be maintained. **If we maintain our current course, I fear we will see a significant drop in the living standards of Developed Countries. I am aiming to maintain the Developed Countries' standards whilst improving the Developing Countries standard as quickly as possible.** I suggest using eight countries to give a fair average which would eliminate any inefficiency in some market sectors among the nations chosen. I suggest discarding the top price of each item, and use an average of the other seven nations; this would reduce the chance of any one country deliberately manipulating prices.

The Sydney Morning Herald reported on 13th February 2013, "China has leapfrogged the US to become the World's biggest trading nation" "It is remarkable that an economy that is only a fraction of the size of the US economy has a larger trading volume"

There are a number of very sophisticated estimating software packages in common use, which would be suited for this purpose. All companies would have their own database of manufacturing time standards. Countries should use the standards from the most efficient companies not merely choose the average. Given the benefits that larger companies in Developed Countries would be likely to get from this system, I am sure they would be happy to provide this information, and assist in establishing the standards. These times, at the average labour rate, together with the bill-of-materials (which shows the materials required to build each sub-assembly), combine to form the basic product cost. There are companies that currently offer an external estimating service, so the mechanism and experience to do this already exists.

In this age of computerisation, modern transportation, and ready access to information buyers have instant access to prices at the local, national, and world level, producers know they have to be as efficient as their competitors or they won't be in the race. Throughout the same geographic area, the standard cost of production for a particular item is fairly uniform (for the same quality), and would not vary greatly among the most developed nations of the World. All industries are becoming more mechanised each year. This would result in a reduction in the cost of labour as a percentage of total cost. Therefore, over a period of several decades, differences in wage rates would become less of a concern. This would make the cost structures of Developed and Developing Countries converge over time. Even products whose production is greatly affected by the climate would not have greatly differing costs. For example, in Australia, sugar farmers get only about one sixth of the final retail value for their crop, so even if their cost of production was 30% higher than Brazil this would only make a 5% difference to the retail price. For these reasons, when we compare the cost of goods of the same quality, I don't think the difference would be as great as one might think.

This system would at first be to the detriment of the Underdeveloped Countries, but I don't believe this would be the case for long. Under the present system they are allowed to produce and sell any old quality—so they do. Under The Fair Dinkum Economy they would soon see that the only way they can continue to participate in the international market place is to ensure their produce meets (or better still exceeds) the new minimum standards. This would drive them to become better skilled and more innovative. I think we would quickly see countries like Indonesia, China, Mexico, Brazil, and India matching and surpassing the quality of the Developed Countries. This in turn would put pressure on the latter to pick up their game, which is after all one of the main aims of the FES. I will examine this concept in more detail later in the book.

The FITP would need to be based on one currency, the United States dollar would be the obvious choice for this as it is already the defacto international currency. Each country would convert these prices to their own currency. This is when things start to get a bit complicated. Exchange rates are continuously changing. It would not be possible to operate this new system if the FITP was continuously changing, so in order to overcome this we would need to lock in prices for say 12 months. Inflation is another factor which would cause costs to change during the year. This is not too different to what companies face now; when contracts are signed, or orders placed, they are based on the prevailing exchange rate and costs. If changes to the exchange rate increase the cost of production then either the supplier, the manufacturer or the customer has to suffer the extra cost (depending on the contract conditions). Inflation can cause the same effect although what usually happens is the producer makes an allowance in his quote. Ideally what I would like to see is all international exchange rates fixed for a period of time (say annually), and inflation conquered—see my thoughts on these matters later in the book. Maybe, in the meantime, there would need to be an allowance for a mid-year adjustment, to be made if the exchange rate fluctuates by more than a certain amount.

FITPs would have to be recalculated at the start of each year, and each year's prices tabulated. This would allow consumers to check them on the Internet (based on the item's year of manufacture).

The estimators made redundant in manufacturing, and the service industry could be redeployed into specialised estimating firms, and government departments who would be responsible for updating, monitoring and enforcing a country's compliance with the new FITP.

Non-standard Manufactured Goods

There are many goods and services which are non-standard and made-to-order such as specialised machinery, buildings, bridges, maintenance service etc. These items would not have a FITP, so they would need a different solution.

With these types of goods the customer requests a tender for a specific design or requirement. The suppliers or contractors then prepare and submit a quote, and the customer accepts whichever one best suit his requirements, and offers the best value for money. Sometimes this is the cheapest, but often it is not, they choose the one that best fits the bill.

There are several problems with this system:

- Customers do not always know exactly what they want. They know they have a need, but the best solution is not always obvious. This often results in them being dissatisfied with the results.
- As mentioned previously, contractors/suppliers have to have considerable estimating resources to prepare their quotes. As only a small percentage of tenders are successful, this substantially increases their overhead cost, which then have to be recouped through higher prices.
- As each quote is different, it is very easy and common for estimators to miss items out of the estimate, or

underestimate the time it will take. Since most jobs are won on small profit margins, any error can have a serious effect on the result, and too many jobs end up at a loss.

- It is not uncommon for contractors/suppliers to go broke in the middle of a contract due to mistakes in their tendering, mismanagement or some other misfortune, leaving the customer with the dilemma of trying to finish the job. In these situations sub-contractors and material suppliers to the prime contractor can suffer high losses as in many cases the contractor does not have the assets to pay all of their outstanding invoices. This leads to much hardship, sometimes sending the sub-contractors also into liquidation.

<u>Let us look at a typical case under the current system:</u>

Company A has just lodged a tender for a job they are keen to win. They know there are at least 5 of their major competitors in the bidding. They, and another competitor, Company B have submitted the best prices. They both notice that there are inconsistencies in the customer's design. Company A works out that it would not take much to correct these, so they just make a small allowance in their tender, but Company B decides to base their strategy on quoting low to win the tender then lodging substantial variation claims for this extra work later on, which would carry a high mark up.

Company A does not have much work booked for the time period when this job would have to be done, so they really need this work. Normally they would aim for 20% mark-up to cover their selling and administration expenses and return a reasonable

94

profit, but as they need the work, they decide to drop it 15%. Their customer rings (trying to screw down their price) to advise them that they are the second lowest quote. They revisit their labour estimates and kid themselves into thinking that they can increase their productivity; they have done similar work before and they figure that they would be more efficient next time. They then ring their sub-contractors and suppliers and manage to get a further 5% reduction off their prices; they also cut their mark-up to 12%. The next day they go back to the customer and reduce their original offer by 10%. The next day the customer rings to advise them that Company B has also reduced their price, and they are 5% cheaper. After much soul searching and wasted management time, Company A finally decides, very sensibly, not to continue the price war.

By the end of the job, with the variation claims submitted by Company B, the customer ends up paying more than Company A's original price. Company B already had a large workload for this period, they had hoped to be able to employ casual labour to do this job, but have had trouble getting the skills they need. They also stretch their supervisors' workload beyond their limit, and mistakes are made which results in high material wastage and rework. The job ends up being delivered 4 weeks late, at great inconvenience to the customer, and Company B is lucky to break-even.

A Better Approach under The Fair Dinkum Economy:

I suggest a change to the traditional approach to tendering, one that should reduce the risk and cost. What I suggest is switching the responsibility around, so it is the customer who prepares the estimate. They could choose to have their own department or engage specialised external estimating firms (either private or government) to prepare the documents.

Materials required for the job would be based on the FITP if the goods are imported, otherwise the estimators would request quotes from local manufacturers, as they do now.

I would like to see the hourly standards for labour and machines controlled by the Government, therefore all firms would use the same base data. This would make it easy for the contractors— they would just have to satisfy themselves once, that they can meet or better the standard times for the relevant tasks. This would save them having to check the hours for each tender they submit they would just need to ensure the number of bricks, welds, cuts etc. are correct. It would also give firms an industry benchmark against which they could compare their performance against their competitors.

Tendering would be done in two stages:-

1. The customer would post the details of the job, their detailed estimate of the cost and the minimum price they are willing to pay, on their Web Site. Approved contractors/suppliers would be able to access this information and submit their interest in doing the work for the price specified or maybe for a higher price (but not lower) if they feel they have a premium service/product to offer. The estimate documents provided by the customers would include a list of conditions that each contractor/supplier would have to meet in order to

be eligible to tender. These would include technical and financial compliance like, quality certifications, safety record, reputation, track record, and proof of financial security. On larger jobs this would immediately reduce the list of potential suppliers to a small select group.

This first stage of tendering should be a cheap and quick process for the contractor. Having previously established that the Government's standard hours for each task were acceptable, they would just have to ensure that the dollar rates per hour are adequate to cover their labour costs and overheads. They would accept the estimated total hours and material quantities at this stage; they would have a chance to check these later if they are the successful tenderer. The only other things they would need to consider is their existing workload for the period concerned and whether they have the resources to do the work in the time required.

2. The customer would then appoint the successful tenderer, on a conditional basis. Now that the contractor/supplier knows that they are the conditional, successful party they would be happy to spend more time in reviewing the estimate in detail. They would firstly need to satisfy themselves that the total number of hours is correct. Having previously verified that the government's standard hour for each task is acceptable, they just now need to ensure that the correct number of tasks has been allowed. For example, assume it is a building job, and they are checking the bricklaying section of the workscope, they have already accepted the standard, that it takes say 36 minutes to lay 100 bricks, and they have checked the dollar rate per hour for labour is acceptable in Stage 1, so

they just need to ensure the estimators have allowed for enough bricks for the job. They don't need to check the material cost as they have fixed quotes from suppliers.

Once the conditional, successful tenderer has satisfied themselves that the estimate is acceptable, they would notify their approval to the customer, and the contract would be finalised. If the feel that something is not right then they would need to discuss it with the customer, and if the customer agrees, the estimate would be adjusted accordingly. Once the estimate is finally approved by the contractor, then any mistakes or omissions would be at the contractor's risk.

If all contractors are offering the same price how would they differentiate themselves from their competitors? They would have to rely on their other qualities such as:

- Their track record (previous experience on similar work).
- Their quality qualifications and systems.
- The quality of the materials they use.
- Their key performance indicators (e.g. success at meeting delivery deadlines, labour turnover, rework percentage, downtime, ratings from customer satisfaction surveys etc).
- Their safety record and statistics.
- Most importantly—advice on improving the design or reducing costs (this would be done in Stage 1).
- Their system for controlling the job (in particular how they track and report progress).
- Their design software.

- The size of their facilities and their list of equipment.
- A list of their sub-contractors.
- The service-life of their products.
- Their after sales service and warranty.
- Their financial strength.
- The skills of their workforce.
- Their managerial strength.
- A list of business partners.
- Commendations from other customers.

Most of this technical data would be the same for all tenders, so it would only have to be prepared once, and then maintained from year-to-year. This would be all that the contractor would needed to submit in their tender, this would reduce their tendering costs to a fraction of what they are, under the current, inefficient system.

Specialised estimating firms would be better organised and controlled than most of the current contractors' estimating teams. They would have a wider range of skills to call on, have more efficient systems, and have stricter checking procedures which would reduce the risk of making mistakes and omissions in tenders.

Now this system may sound a bit radical, and some of you may be wondering if customers would accept estimates that had not been tested by competitively tendering? Most customers are willing to pay a reasonable price for a job well done. If they could trust the supplier/contractor to do the right thing and charge an honest price for their services then there would be less need for competitive tendering. Unfortunately there are some people who cannot be trusted to do the right thing. Customers have grown accustomed to being very cautious, hence their desire to get multiple tenders. However this is not always the case, there are many jobs which are settled on a "do-and-charge" or "cost-plus" basis. These methods are usually used in instances where it is not possible to estimate a final price as the cost will not be known until the job is well underway. For this to work there must be a high level of trust between the parties concerned which would have resulted either from a long-term relationship or a recommendation from colleagues. The supplier/contractor appreciates the benefits of this type of arrangement, it saves them the cost and risk of preparing estimates and guarantees them all that type of work, from that customer, so they will not do anything to jeopardise it. An example of this type of work would be where a contractor has an arrangement for the long-term repair of a customer's equipment; they often will not know how much work is involved in the repair until they disassemble the equipment. With this method of pricing the customer does not have a fixed price; they just agree to pay all costs plus a reasonable margin.

Many contractors/suppliers (particularly smaller ones) do not do not have the skills to prepare accurate quotes, particularly if they are looking to diversify. Also they have been conditioned by the FES to engage in price-cutting wars which, as we have seen in previous chapters of this book, are often fatal for their business.

The Fair Dinkum Economy has the promise of reducing the risk of running a business which would benefit the economy and community as a whole—more stable jobs, fewer company failures and lower bad debts. This would lead to reduced costs for both the customer and contractor/supplier.

A Fairer Deal for Farmers

In Australia, up to the 1970s farming used to be a prosperous industry. The land was divided into smaller lots, and even medium-sized farms used to be able to support two or three families. Farmers used to get a good return for their efforts; they lived a hard, but comfortable life, and were able to set funds aside for the bad years, which they knew would sometimes come. The days of small farms has now disappeared, many farms have been acquired, and merged by larger companies, over the years more and more of these are owned by overseas countries. Small farmers have to acquire two or three other farms, if they can afford it, to become a viable size. Over the last 20 years 40% of farm workers have left the industry. The remaining family farms are struggling to support one family. The average farm annual income is lucky to be positive let alone above the minimum wage. Many farm workers have been forced to take a second job in town or in the mines in order to pay their bills. This is a ridiculous situation, which can't be allowed to continue!

The farming sector in Developed Countries is under great threat from the FES, Globalisation, and more recently Climate Change. They are unique in terms of the risks they take and the problems they face. Their cost structure is largely dependent on external factors like drought, flood, fire, hail, frost, storms, temperature, predators, pests, vermin, and disease over which they have little control. Farmers are under threat from the dumping of surplus foreign produce into their domestic market and the pressure from large national conglomerates to lower their prices. Sometimes this means their farms are no longer viable, and the farmer is forced to sell. This is a great skill loss to the Country, and is very unfair on families whom in many cases have been on their land for several generations.

A friend of mine owned a large sheep and dairy farm in a very fertile valley. The farm had been in their family for several generations. They were forced to sell, not through any fault of their own, but because wool and dairy had become unprofitable. Their demise happened very quickly over a ten year period, they could do nothing to stop it, and the family was devastated. The new owner turned it into a horse stud; it seems consumers are willing to pay anything for gambling and drugs, but not for essentials like food.

In 2005 a newspaper report (The Herald, 22nd Oct) revealed that Riverland citrus growers were saying that their industry faced collapse as companies such as Berri were using imported fruit juice concentrate from Brazil. Thousands of tonnes of fruit had to be thrown away as it could not be sold, and some orange growers did not even bother to pick their crop.

The whole population of the World relies on a regular supply of farming products for their very survival. **I therefore feel that it is only fair that the whole of society should carry the risk that farming encompasses.** The question then is how can we best spread this risk? Farmers are the caretakers of much of our land, they get very little acknowledgement of this, and even less assistance, they should be subsidised for their part in preserving our environment. In order to maintain their yields farmers are forced to kill stock predators like eagles, dingos, tigers, foxes, and animals and birds that eat their crops. In spraying their crops for pests they also kill "good" insects and beneficial micro-bacteria, and unintentionally, other animals higher up the food chain. If society wants to save endangered animals and the diversity of life then it must accept that part of the price they will have to pay is that there will be a higher amount of spoilage of farm produce, but farmers should be compensated for their losses, so they are not out of pocket.

Consumers often pay high prices for low grade food in the off-season then low prices when things are plentiful and good quality. Consumers usually don't know what quality they are buying because the grading is poor or non-existent. The look does not indicate the taste, a tomato or strawberry can be bright red with unblemished skin, but when you eat it, there is just no flavour—this should not, and does not, have to be the case. What we need is a system where the farmer is paid a fixed amount for his efforts and consumers pay the same price for the goods all year (when available). Notice I said "efforts"—this means the farmer would still be paid, even if something happens outside of their control. This would guarantee the farmer a regular income the same as a store owner, a factory worker or a CEO.

How can this work?

- I suggest setting up a non-profit government marketing body to buy all the produce. This body would perform a similar function as the existing Australian Wool Marketing and Wheat Marketing Boards, but with a different pricing policy. This body would set the price to be paid to the farmers, and handle the on-selling to the wholesalers. There would be a FITP for all imported produce that would include all the normal direct costs of farming as well as things like purchasing water during the drought years, long-term sustainability costs (like pasture improvement, capital equipment investment, and replacement), an allowance for spoilage (including that from the reduced use of pesticides), and good farm-management costs (like business planning and breeding programs). A mark-up would then be added to the costs. This should mean that local produce would be about the same price as the imported produce—i.e. the FITP. Consumers then would decide whether to buy local or imported, based on the quality of the food. This competition would result in an improvement in the taste. If price and quality are equal then consumers would undoubtedly buy from domestic producers, and only buy the imported goods when there is no local supply, and that would be a good thing.

- For crops—farmers would register their interest with the marketing body stating what they would be planting and what tonnage they would expect to produce, under good conditions, based on their experience. The marketing body would know from historical data what the demand would be. At the beginning of the season they would allocate an allowance to each farm based on the size of their registered crop, taking a spoilage allowance into account. They would specify a certain minimum quality standard of nutrition and taste which would be the same used in arriving at the FITP. The farmers would be required to commit to an agreed delivery date. The farmer probably would only plant a sufficient area to meet their allowance. They could decide to plant more, but there would be no guarantee that they would be able to sell the surplus—it would depend on the season and yields from other areas.

- For stock—the system would be basically the same as for crops, but the farmers would register to supply a certain number of head of a set quality, and deliver at an agreed time, again for a set minimum price.

- If all goes well then the farmer just has to deliver the agreed quantity of goods on time, and as long as the quality is acceptable they would be paid the agreed price. If growing/breeding conditions turn out to be worse than average (for previous years) or there is a natural disaster (like flood, insect plague, drought or fire) which effects the quantity or quality of their produce then there needs to be a mechanism whereby they can apply for an increase in their spoilage allowance. In order for the farmer to be granted this extra adversity allowance, the marketing body would do an audit to verify the extent of the damage, and that the farmer had done all in their power to minimise their losses.

- Let's take the example of a wheat crop, say the contract had been for 1,000 tonnes, and that the average rainfall during the growing season is 250mm. If the rainfall was only 200mm, and the farmer could not supply their allocation, they could apply for an adversity allowance of 20% of the contracted amount, so they would only need to deliver 800 tonnes, but would be paid for the full contract value. If they fail to supply the agreed amount (after taking spoilage into account) then they would only be paid proportionally. In the example above, if they only supplied 600 tonnes instead of the 800, they would only be paid 75% (600/850) of the total contract value.

- In the good years farm production volumes would probably be greater than average, and this would lead to a surplus over and above the contract quantity. The marketing body would have the option of buying this surplus, but this would depend on demand, the shelf-life of the product, and the available storage. The farmer would be paid at a lower unit price for this surplus because they would have already covered their fixed costs (like equipment leasing, depreciation, interest, fertiliser, permanent labour, water) as part of his normal capacity allowance. The marketing body would sell all produce at the same price which would give them extra profit on the surplus quantity. This would enable them to create a reserve fund to cover the bad years.

- If a farmer does not meet their contract quantity (after taking the spoilage allowance into account) then their contract quantity would be reduced for the next season.
- There would probably need to be some kind of bonus paid to the farmer if the quality of their produce is higher than the minimum, and the marketing body would pass this cost onto the wholesalers in the form of a premium on the normal price (remembering that the FITP is also a minimum, not fixed).
- Contracted quantities would have to be adjusted over time depending on changes in demand (e.g. a substitute product may become more in demand like margarine for butter), and to allow for growers leaving or entering the market. This may require farmers to look for alternative goods to produce.

Now there is sure to be some hard years when this marketing body would run at a loss (like the 7 year drought Australia experienced from 2003 to 2010), and not have the reserves to cover it. In such instances their losses would be subsidised from the Government's general revenue, but that is alright—this is how the weather-risk would be shared by all the taxpayers.

The marketing body would usually sell at the FITP, but surplus perishable goods, which can't be preserved, would be sold at whatever price was needed to try and dispose of the remainder of the stock (see section on Surplus Stock for details).

To the consumer this would generally mean consistent prices all year round. In season, a particular foodstuff would be supplied by local producers, in other months it may be imported, and yet at other times there may be no supplies at all; we would still be much better served than our grandparents. We may have to pay more for our foodstuffs, more in line with what was paid in the middle of the last century (after allowing for inflation), but the nutrition and taste would return to our food. Studies in 2005 show that in Australia, households wasted $5.3 billion of food, 25% ended up in our rubbish bins. We may just have to learn to be more frugal with what we buy, and make sure we used up those left-overs.

Decentralisation

In all countries the majority of the population live in major cities which occupy only a small percentage of the land. Their residents have to travel long distances to get to work wasting precious time and fuel. In Developed Countries many families in the larger cities have two or three cars which leads to more congestion on the roads, lower productivity, and much time wasted. Other negative aspects of large cities are much higher house prices, increases in air pollution, and higher crime rates. Governments are keen to encourage more people to decentralise, and move into regional areas to live, but without a lot of success.

The Fair Dinkum Economy would revitalise country areas, breathing life back into local agriculture and the communities that support it. Higher prices and a guaranteed income for domestic producers would once again make it viable for many products to be locally made. Farmers would again be able to grow oranges where there were once abundant orchards, vegetables, and milk would be grown and supplied locally instead of being brought in from other states or overseas. Wool and wheat industries would once again thrive in Australia. Manufacturers would be attracted to these areas because of the cheaper rent and wages. This would result in the growth of a myriad of industries like furniture and clothing manufacturers. Workers would be attracted by the easier and better lifestyle, and cheaper housing. Increases in the populations of country towns would justify building better health and community facilities, and improving roads and railways.

One of the major deterrents to people and businesses decentralising is that goods are more expensive in the regional areas as they have to be transported over larger distances. What I would like to see is a country-wide average freight allowance in the FITP which would be sufficient to cover delivery to, and from remote areas. This would mean a small increase in the price paid by city consumers, but it would not be significant.

Monitoring Compliance

As I have said, if this system is to work it would take the support of all countries. Each country would also have to agree to enforce compliance. They would need to establish a Review Committee to ensure that all imports met the required quality standards, and goods are not sold below the FITP. They would carry out random audits on suppliers' prices and have the appropriate power to penalise companies who break the law, and de-register those that continue to do so.

The Review Committee would rely on community surveillance to assist them in monitoring quality. The quality standards established by the G8 Group Pricing Committee would be posted on the Internet, and local companies and consumers would be asked to dob in (Australian for "inform on") any retailer selling below this quality and price. I would expect a smart-phone App would be written to make it easy for consumers to check the standards. Better still, an RFID microchip scanners could be built into the mobile phone. A quick scan of the item would bring up all its FITP and quality standards. Software would be written to allow consumers to readily send a SMS/Facebook/ Twitter message to report any infringements.

The Pricing Committee would also have to play a monitoring role, and even have to power to ban a particular country from international trading for a period of time if their exporters continue to sell non-complying goods. This would encourage all exporting countries to monitor the quality of their exports to avoid a country-wide ban. They could, for example, set-up a licensing system for their exporting companies which would be subject to an audit, similar to that now operating with international quality standards.

The Effect on the Developing Countries

I am sure that people living in a Developing Country, would much prefer to have a job that paid a reasonable wage, rather than relying on charity to live. I think everybody wants to feel useful; they want to feel they are contributing to life in a meaningful way. Just giving the poor money may keep them alive (as long as the money keeps coming), but it does nothing for their self-esteem, and little to improve their standard of living. We need to teach them the skills they need to do worthwhile jobs, and let them share equitably, in the wealth they help to generate.

Initially, under The Fair Dinkum Economy, Developing Countries would lose some export business, until they make the changes necessary to meet the new standards. If they are selling goods to a country where there is no local producer then their exports would continue. As the cost of their goods would increase the quantity sold may drop (depending on the elasticity of demand for that particular product), but their income should increase. If however they are selling to a country where they are competing with local producers, their exports would decline, and maybe even cease. Then they would have to work hard at improving their products, and they would need good marketing strategies.

If they are manufacturers, they would no longer be able to get by just making poor copies of other countries' ideas. They would need to get more involved in research and development, and continuous improvement programs to differentiate their product and increase quality. Remember, the FITP is the minimum price; companies are free to charge more if they can justify the higher quality and better features of their product. There is no reason why, given time, they could not be just as competitive as the Developed Countries. As they improve their training, the quality of the raw materials they use, and their quality control systems, their wage rates would increase, and their suppliers would be able to charge higher prices for the better quality materials they provide. The improvements to exported products would also result in improvements to the goods produced for local consumption. These factors would lead to an increase in that country's standard of living.

Let's look in more detail at what the effect may be:

<u>An example—a drill:</u>

Company A is a manufacturer in a Developed Country of a battery powered, hand drill. Company B is a manufacturer in a Developing Country of a copy of Company A's drill. Both companies have been exporting drills to the same customer, Company C, in another Developed Country. Company B's drills are 1/3rd the price of Company A's, but a much lower quality. Company A has been steadily losing sales since Company B started in the market 10 years ago as many consumers won't pay more for quality!

Once The Fair Dinkum Economy commences Company B's export price would increase substantially to be the same as all other competing countries. Company C's customers would now be faced with the option of buying Company A's or Company B's drills for the same price—what would happen?

Company A's exports would increase, so they would be very happy, their prospects for the future look rosy now that they can be assured of a guaranteed price for their drills. This would encourage them to invest, employ more labour, and grow their business—reversing their downward slide.

Company B on the other hand would start to lose business. They would quickly need to bring their quality up to meet the new international standard. They could just choose to concentrate on their own local domestic market, but this would greatly limit their growth as the big consumers are in the Developed Countries. They would undoubtedly choose to improve. As their cost-base is lower, they would have a much higher profit margin per item. This would also give them the financial advantage and incentive to invest in better machinery, and start paying higher wages to attract the best skilled labour available. They would have a hard time initially, convincing their export customers that they can produce a superior product, but I am confident they would succeed in time—just look at the progress Japan managed to achieve in the 30 years after World War II, and that was starting with a devastated economy.

<u>Another hypothetical example—oranges:</u>

A is a Developing Country which has an ideal climate for growing oranges. It exports its oranges to two Developed Countries, B and C. Country B cannot grow oranges as its climate is not suitable. Country C can grow them, but its farmers can't compete with the price of the imports, and their domestic industry is dying. The imported oranges look good, but the quality and taste varies with each shipment.

Under The Fair Dinkum Economy the prices of imported oranges would increase. Consumers in Country B would continue to buy them because they have no choice, but the volume of sales would be expected to drop. As Country A would be getting a higher price for their produce they would be able to afford to invest in improving the taste of their crop and making the quality more consistent—which would greatly please their consumers.

Country C's farmers have always grown better tasting fruit, and now that it is the same price as imports, they would have all the business during the growing season. Country A would still get sales out-of-season, but the quality would be greatly reduced.

Even though Country A would initially lose sales they would not suffer as much as you may at first think . . . .

A was selling:-

10,000 tonnes to B @ $1,000 per tonne

and

10,000 tonnes to C @ $1,000 per tonne

If their cost of goods sold is $900 per tonne they make—>

20,000 x (1,000—900) = $2 M profit.

Under the new system the FITP is set at $1,400 per tonne, a 40% increase on A's price.

A has to improve its quality to meet the new standard, so its costs go up to $1,200 per tonne. With better quality fruit, the level of its sales to B falls by only 20%, but sales to C dropped by 80%.

What would A's profit now be?

Sales would be:

8,000 tonnes to B @ $1,400 per tonne

and

2,000 tonnes to C @ $1,400 per tonne

Profit would be:

10,000 x (1,400 - 1,200) = $2 M profit.

Country A's profit per tonne has increased from $100 to $200. They would make the same total profit, with only half the sales and effort. They would be better off as they would have increased the skills and wages of their workers, updated machinery, and hopefully made their environment more sustainable.

The Effect on the Developed Countries

As we have discussed, there is much uncertainly in Developed Countries about the future of their economy, their jobs and their standard of living. Company closures have been so widespread that most families have been either directly affected or have close relatives and friends whom have been retrenched.

Under The Fair Dinkum Economy, companies would no longer be continually losing jobs and market share to overseas competition; they would be able to plan ahead with certainty, knowing that any investment would have long-term benefits. They would be willing to increase spending on training to ensure a reliable source of skilled labour for the future. For the last 20 years Australian companies have been reducing the number of apprentices they train. Recently training institutions have been cutting courses in vital areas like metallurgy, welding, creative arts, and aeronautical engineering; this decline should be reversed under this system.

One major benefit would be that the quality and service-life of goods would improve. Over time this would have the effect of reducing a company's sales as items would not have to be replaced as often, but as companies would now be paid a higher, fairer price, and are not having to engage in price wars, their profit margins would increase, and this is the true measure of success.

With more work and job assurance the financial institutions would be more willing to lend to companies and employees. People would start buying houses again, safe in the knowledge that their future is secure.

An example—trains:

Some years ago a local company in my town was awarded a government contract to make a number of passenger trains. In order to reduce their cost they bought some of their components from overseas. They had many quality problems with the material used in the manufacture, and had to spend extra time on the assembly. This led to very late delivery and a very unhappy customer. The Government had to keep using old rolling stock which they had planned to replace; these kept breaking down and were blamed for many disruptions to rail services much to the chagrin of passengers. In addition to this there was a more component failure in service which increased warranty costs. The manufacturer ended up losing money on this contract. Now you could say that that was their fault for risking the use of components from unproven, overseas suppliers, but I think it was really Globalisation which was to blame. The company had little choice, they had to either try using cheaper parts from overseas in their tender or not win the job—probably the whole contract would then have been awarded to an overseas competitor.

Note also that the local component manufacturers who missed supplying this contract would have had to downsize, and in some cases close.

Under the Fair Dinkum Economy the price of trains would increase which would allow local manufacturers to continue using Australian components. Had this system have been in place at the time the original contract was awarded the manufacturer would have had fewer problems, probably delivered on time, and made a profit. Did Globalisation result in a lower ticket price for commuters—I guess we will never know, but I suspect not!

The Need to Change Companies' Attitudes

The success of The Fair Dinkum Economy depends on the support of the Government, the public, and the business community. Hopefully companies will recognise the benefits they would receive, and give the necessary support to ensure its smooth introduction. Company Boards would need to put more emphasis on their social responsibility to the community that supports them. Some of these changes would be hard for directors to digest, but I feel confident it would prove to be to their benefit.

Once you take price out of the decision to buy, buyers would start to look more closely at other factors. Quality and service would become paramount, and these depend on the attitude and commitment of the front-line workers. The companies that treat their employees well, and show concern for their well-being would be the ones that emerge the most successful out of this fairly radical change.

Over the last two decades there has been a major change in the way progressive companies treat their customers and suppliers. They have realised that if they work together, in partnership, they can create win-win deals and strategic alliances which maximise the benefits to all parties. Business relationships should be based on mutual respect and the desire for both parties to profit, and get something out of the relationship. Unfortunately, under the FES, competitors are still out there trying to beat each other to death. It would be great if companies could better share the market and be satisfied with a good return, and smaller growth. Every religion in the World preaches "do unto others as you would have done to you" or words to that effect. They all support the concept of showing compassion to their fellow man, but this is not being followed by most companies in free-trade economies.

Companies in big cities can learn a lot from their farming brothers—two neighbours working on adjoining properties—competitors—they socialise together—they are always there for each other when needed in times of flood, accident, sickness, any adversity—they lend each other equipment—they belong to the same church—they sit on the same committees—they are happy just to earn a good honest living, and are pleased to see their friends doing the same. In recent catastrophic bush fires in Australia, which devastated hundreds of thousands of hectares of farmland, we saw farmers from other States sending equipment and feed to assist their fellow farmers.

What does it take to make a strong and good company?

- the fair treatment of their workers and business partners
- a real emphasis on customer service.
- healthy and fair competition in the market
- recognition of the value of quality
- a high level of innovation
- a continuous improvement program
- a policy of long-term planning for sustainability
- a commitment to protect the environment
- being a good corporate citizen
- the complete support of this policy by top management

What is wrong with companies' attitudes under the current system?

The Quest for never-ending growth:

Why do companies feel the need for continual growth? Why do they have to continue acquiring other companies? Capitalism is based on the concept of accumulating wealth and making people richer. This encourages people to work and think harder to achieve their goals, and this is fine. Growing sales often relies on a growing population which is not good for the planet. Why can't entrepreneurs and shareholders be satisfied with a reasonable return on their investment; why can't a company stop growing once it has reached this point—I guess that is when we see the ugly side of capitalism—greed. I have seen a number of companies suffer because of their emphasis on growth, instead of curing their existing problems they are too busy acquiring new businesses or taking on larger contracts than they can manage. This leads to increased employee stress, more mistakes, rework, and poorer quality jobs. This in turn results in damage to their reputation, a higher staff turnover, a lack of continuous improvement, and in extreme cases the demise of the company. It takes a long time to build a company's culture, when they acquire other companies; it gets partially degraded and takes a long time to re-build. Assimilation of new employees takes a long time and a lot of effort. If companies are continually growing and buying—up competitors businesses, they will never be able to build the culture to which they should aspire.

The excessive remuneration of CEOs:

The other alarming trend is the growth in the salaries of Chief Executive Officers (CEOs), in 1965 American CEOs were paid 20 times the average wage, in 2011 that figure was estimated to be 231 times . . . . this has happened in just 60 years—nobody is that good. The Prime Minister of Australia (the highest office) gets paid AUD$ 500,000 per annum plus allowances which are only seven times the average wage. A farmer would have to invest about $ 2 million to buy and set-up a broadacre farm. They invest their life savings, work ridiculous hours, have no one to support them if they get sick or have an accident, and risk losing everything they own if the weather is against them. According to the Australian Bureau of Agricultural and Resource Economics and Sciences, in 2011 the average farm income was $ 82,000, and that was a good year! Not a very good return on investment is it? Compare that to a CEO of a large corporation, they do work long hours, but they have a large team to support them, they carry no personal finance risk (apart from the shares in the company which have usually been given to them as part of their salary package), and are covered with insurance if they get sick—a bit unfair don't you think? I have worked with some of these high profile executives, and some of the decisions they make are disastrous; just like the rest of us—they make mistakes. They are quick to take the credit when a decision works out for the better, but you rarely hear about the bad ones.

Much of the CEO's income is performance-based rewards, but it is easy for unscrupulous CEOs to manipulate the system to maximise their bonuses. If you offer a manager millions of dollars in bonus for achieving some singular target (like the percentage increase in sales or the return on funds employed), then who could blame them if that becomes the main driver of their decision making. I have seen instances, where a manager's salary incentive has resulted in action, which was to the detriment of their peers, and damaging to the longer-term performance of their company. If you follow the careers of these executives you will find that often, the same CEO who presides over a brilliant result in one company (and takes the credit), is soon reporting a large drop in profit at the next company they work for—just because they get paid like they are super-human, does not mean they are. Of course there are always plenty of excuses, other than their performance—how much did these large salary packages contribute to the losses?

On 19th January 2013, The Sydney Morning Herald reported that Rio Tinto, the Anglo-Australian mining giant, had dumped its CEO, Tom Albanese over problems relating to a coal project in Mozambique. Mr Albanese had been paid a base salary of $10.6 million per year for the 5 years he had worked for them He also held $16.7 million in shares, a further $ 16.2 million in share options, and he was expected to get a $2.4 million performance bonus for the 2009 financial year. He had not received any short-term performance bonuses for the previous 2 years results. In addition to this salary he had a pension worth $ 722,000 a year.

In February 2013 another mining giant BHP Billiton announced that their CEO, Marius Kloppers, would be leaving the company. Mr Kloppers had been overseeing several failed takeover bids by BHP Billiton over the last few years which had been a very costly exercise. Their first half profit to December 2012 fell by 58%. In 2009, during a resources boom caused by rapid growth in China, he received a 50% increase in his remuneration to $US 10.4 million.

Following the collapse of the banks at the start of the 2008 Global Financial Crises, it was disclosed that large bonuses had been paid to banking executives, clearly after they knew their business was about to go under! If large companies do well it is because of the combined efforts of their entire workforce. If the CEO is good, at selecting their team, a good motivator, and a good delegator (which is a rare combination of talents), they usually do well, but surely 20 times the average wage would be adequate reward for these skills and the time they contribute. Please note my disparaging remarks above do not apply to all CEOs, there are some excellent ones out there, but I am questioning the extent of their remuneration after all how many millions in savings does it take to live comfortably when you retire.

I am not blaming the CEOs for these ridiculous salaries it is the Companies' Boards of Directors and ultimately the Shareholders who determine their salary packages. This will turn around to bite the wealthy and the economy if something is not done to reverse this inequality—maybe it already is.

"Having more money doesn't make you happier. I have $50 Million, and I am just as happy as when I had $48 Million"—Arnold Schwarzenegger.

The declining distribution of wealth in Developed Countries:

In America, the change in the distribution of wealth over the last 35 years has been outrageous. Since 1978 the proportion of the Country's income held by the wealthiest 10% of the population has grown astronomically . . . . at the expense of the lower income earners. The richest 400 people now have as much wealth as the poorest 150 million! In other words with 315 million people in that Country, the richest 400 people control as much wealth as 48% of the population. In many Developed

Countries the wealthiest income earners pay a lower percentage of tax than the low income workers—this needs to be fixed. In Australia for example there is a 10% tax on capital gain, and in America it is 15% which is a large part of the income of the wealthy sector each year.

In theory Globalisation should be delivering major benefits to people living in Developing Countries. The benefits are not being shared as they should be; the financial gains have largely gone into the pockets of large business and government.

It is time the World got serious about poverty, I fully support the basic principle of Capitalism that if people have the adequate drive and ability, they should have the opportunity to succeed and earn a high income. There needs to be a large difference between the top and bottom wages as an incentive for people to work hard, increase their skills and take risks, but this has gotten out of control in modern day Developed Countries. America is the most affluent nation in the World yet is has a high level of poverty and child mortality (nearly twice as high as the United Kingdom, and four times higher than Japan); not a record to be proud of, and it has gotten worse over the last 20 years. According to the National Centre for Children in Poverty in Columbia "nearly 15 million children in the United States—21% of all children—live in families with incomes below the federal poverty level—$22,350 a year for a family of four. Most of these children have parents who work".

In recent years we have seen the beginning of a very generous movement by Billionaires to donate substantial parts of their fortunes to charity, and scientific and medical research. Whilst there have always been large philanthropists such as the Rockefeller Family, they were rare. Bill and Melinda Gates set an example in 1994 when they donated hundreds of millions of dollars of their fortunes to medical research and reducing world poverty. In 2010 they banded together with Warren Buffet to set up "The Giving Pledge"—this is a commitment by currently 92 billionaires to donate half of their fortunes to medical research and charity. Many of these people own their own business, but there is also a number of CEOs among them. Now while this is to be highly commended, I feel it is like patching holes in the fabric of life. Would we not be better off to make the cloth stronger in the first place by giving the poor the opportunities and means to fend for themselves—if I was in their shoes (the poor) that is certainly what I would prefer.

I believe that companies should exist primarily to serve their employees and their customers. If they do this then they deserve to, and probably will thrive and the owners/shareholders will benefit. Let us not lose our sense of purpose.

This system should result in a substantial increase in the quality of goods, so there would be very few failures and warranty claims. This would provide the opportunity to change what I see, as one of the craziest things about our current retail system—the need for customers to physically return faulty goods. Why should the customer spend <u>their</u> time and money, when they were not the cause of the problem? This practice probably started in the days when there were few (or no) telephones, and you had to return to the store to make a claim. What I would like to see is a new system whereby producers do home-visits to fix or replace warranty claims. This would be very welcome by consumers, and would be a huge incentive for producers to ensure they maintain a high and consistent quality.

It is said by some that big business is more powerful than government, and that it is big business that really runs Developed Countries—what do you think?

Superseded, Slow-moving and Perishable Stock

There would need to be some provision made to handle superseded, slow-moving, and perishable stock.

Superseded:

Once a new version or model of a product is introduced and available, nobody is going to want to buy the old version unless it is substantially discounted; therefore, stores need to be able to reduce their price to dispose of the remaining stock. Customers and auditors would be able to find the version number on the identification microdot, customers to make sure they were buying the latest version, and auditors to ensure the price was not reduced before time.

Slow-moving:

Taste and fashion change rapidly. In the clothing industry, for example, fads come and go in a season; we need to have a provision for disposing of stock when demand subsides. Originally, Sales were used to dispose of old left-over stock, but these days a lot of stores have sales as soon as the goods arrive in their store—this is a ridiculous practice. My suggestion would be that once an item is more than 12 months old (based on the date of manufacture on the identification microdot), sellers could reduce its price.

As the FITP is the minimum standard, there would be a large price range in the goods being sold under the same FITP item code. For instance, let's say we have a code for a "dress". The associated quality standard would specify; the minimum quality of cloth, thread, buttons, and zips; the required technique of sewing seams and hems, and attaching buttons; the colour fastness. Say there are two dresses, the first is a basic design, intended for everyday use, and just complies with the minimum standards. The second may be an evening gown by an exclusive designer, made of silk with pleats, lace and sequins. They both would have the same FITP code, but the first dress would have the minimum FITP price, of say $150, while the second may sell for $800. The storekeeper would have to wait for 12 months from the date of manufacture to discount the first dress, but the second one could be reduced to any price above $150 at any time.

Perishable items:

The FITP only applies to imported goods, and as most imported foodstuffs would be in jars or tins, dehydrated, concentrated or stored in refrigeration, they would have long lives. I would suggest a period of 6 months before imported foodstuffs could be discounted.

I envisage that, in Developed Countries, most of the fresh local produce would also be sold at the FITP. There would be no point in domestic sellers discounting their produce below this price as consumers always would choose "local" over "imported" if the price was the same. The sale of this produce would be controlled by the centralised marketing body (see Chapter on Farming), and the only time they would discount would be if they needed to move surplus stock.

The Frustration of Fluctuating Foreign Exchange

A country's exchange rate changes, based on the supply and demand for its currency. I will not pretend to understand the forces at work in the Foreign Exchange Markets, but I would like to highlight some of the negative effects on our economy and their impact on the operation of the Free Enterprise System. I am hoping that this may stimulate some discussion among those in the know who do have some influence over it.

Let me give you 2 examples:

The first—George, a friend of mine, had organised to go to the US in November 2008. He had paid for his airfare when the AUD was 0.96 USD. Three months after he made these plans our dollar had dropped to 0.64, he was devastated. He had saved $AUD10,000 for expenses, now it was going to cost him $AUD15,000, which forced him to borrow the rest. He asked me "how can this happen? There have been no wars or serious natural disasters, and the Australian economy was doing well . . . much better than the US. It appeared that just because some 'financial wizards' have loaned money unwisely, 10,000 kilometres away, I have to pay 50% more for my holiday"! At this time the World was in recession, it was the start of the "Global Financial Crises", but the Australian economy was faring better than practically any other country, so why the big drop? The reason was (and this is the problem with floating exchange rates), simply peoples' perceptions. Like the share markets, foreign exchange rates vary based on investors' fears and expectations which are heavily influenced by the very, bias opinions of so-called "experts".

The second—we all know the devastating effect that a strengthening of a country's currency, against that of its principal trading partners, can have. It makes the country's exports more expensive, and if the change is prolonged, it has the power to devastate an industry. It does mean that imports will be cheaper, but this too is detrimental to parts of the economy, namely local producers who compete with these imports. In 2012, a large aluminium manufacturer in Australia closed their factory in a small country town, and sacked 400 skilled workers; they were the main employer in the town. They said this was due to a decline in exports caused by the strong Australian dollar. Over a period of 4 years, the AUD had gone from $.64 to $ 1.08 compared to the US$.

How can we expect companies to invest hundreds of millions of dollars needed to build a major piece of plant with this kind of uncertainty? You can't go opening, and closing factories every year on the whim of the financial markets.

Surely there must be a better way. In Australia, up to 1983 we had an exchange rate which was fixed and regulated by the Federal Government. After World War II the whole World

operated on a system called the "Fixed Exchange Rate" which was aimed at stabilising international economies; this system lasted up to the 1970s, so it is possible . . . . I will leave you with those thoughts.

Can Inflation be Eliminated?

The more I studied the problems of our economy, the more I realised how much inefficiency is caused by inflation. What is this inflation, and why does it happen—I do not understand the need for it? Why is it necessary to keep continually increasing wages and prices? It is a vicious circle, prices go up, so workers want an increase in wages in order to maintain their lifestyle; increased wages will lead to increased costs for producers, forcing them to increase their prices to maintain their profits, and so-on and so-forth.

Each time prices rise, there is an enormous administration cost in updating catalogues, price tickets on shelves, prices on Websites, re-doing advertisements, and re-doing company and government budgets and plans. Each time wages increase there are rounds of negotiations, strikes, awards to be updated and statistics to be maintained. Increased wages push us into a higher tax bracket, so we end up paying more tax . . . . until the Government gets around to revising their schedules (and that does not happen too often). When companies estimate new work, they only guarantee the price for a certain period (usually less than a month). Longer-term contracts need to have provision for cost increases, failure to do so will result in reduced profit. This means customers can never be sure exactly what their final cost will be until the end of the job. All this extra paperwork and negotiating is a sheer waste of many people's time for no real benefit that I can see. In our time-deprived world, I am certain people could find more productive ways to use the extra time. Nobody can know what cost, inflation adds to our economy. I bet the total cost to all the World's economies would be more each year, than the Gross National Product of several small countries.

Why must we endure inflation? No inflation, it sounds good doesn't it—is it possible? Maybe the introduction of a new international trading system is a good excuse and time to make radical changes. Let us fantasize for a moment about how this can be achieved. It would be announced that from the introduction of the FITP system, international trade prices would not change, and World Exchange Rates would be fixed. This would force every country to consider ending their domestic inflation. If a country decides to do nothing about inflation, then they would soon reach the stage, where their costs would be too high for them to trade internationally. Each country that wanted to continue to trade internationally would have to pass legislation ending inflation from a date which would be the same date the FITP was to commence. From the time of an individual country's announcement to the inflation-end date, domestic wages and prices would only be allowed to increase by the same percentage as the change in the Consumer Price Index (CPI) during that interval. From this time on there would be no need to change prices regularly, as the cost of materials, components, overheads and wages would not change (except for irregular changes as discussed in the next paragraph).

After the inflation-end date, some prices and wages would still be allowed to change, but only if it was due to factors such as: a change in the quantities used in the manufacture (e.g. a particular process may become more mechanised); a change in the materials used (e.g. improving the grade or quality of steel used in the manufacture); a change in the design (e.g. from TVs using LCD screens rather than cathode ray tubes); an increase in the skills required to do a particular job due to changes in technology (e.g. car mechanics that need extra training to service complex modern engines). In some cases, this would result in prices dropping (e.g. Computers may come down in price due to the development of cheaper/smaller components). These changes would be a lot less frequent than those currently caused by inflation, and would have to be justified to, and approved by the central authority.

The other reason prices fluctuate is due to supply and demand, this would also change. The current theory is, if supply is greater than demand, prices would fall, and this would increase demand to meet supply and vice versa; supply stays the same (at least in the short-term). Under The Fair Dinkum Economy the reverse would apply, prices would be fixed. This would mean supply would be the factor which would have to change, demand would stay the same. Therefore, producers would have to keep an exceptionally close watch on demand, and regulate their production accordingly. The exception to this would be agriculture, and I have discussed this in a previous chapter on Farming.

Can Patents be made Redundant?

My son, Peter, owns a small manufacturing business which makes automated book registration and sorting machines for libraries which he and his business partner invented. They were discussing the need and cost of patents, and this got me thinking about what effect The Fair Dinkum Economy would have on patents. Patent laws were written to protect an inventor's design from being copied, for a certain period of time. The intention was that this would give the inventors several years to recoup their research and development costs, and make good initial profits as a reward for their efforts and initiative, before the competition started to drive prices down. Patents are very expensive, and small inventors often can't afford them. They are also expensive to enforce, and the uncertainty and degree of difficulty of doing so, often turns companies off trying. In this day and age they don't provide full international protection anyway—look at recent cases involving Apple, Samsung, Nokia, and Microsoft.

I believe setting an FITP would eliminate the need for patents. Copiers of a particular design would have to sell on the international market at the same price as the original product— why would a consumer buy a copy, of potentially inferior quality and reliability, when they could buy the original for the same price? As soon as the new invention is ready to sell, companies would apply for a FITP determination; this service would be free. The price would initially include an allowance for the recovery of their development costs, amortised (spread) over a period of say 5 years, then the price would have to be adjusted in line with on-going production costs (i.e. excluding the development). Competitors would be free to copy the design, but this would take time. By the time the copies make it onto the market, the originating company would have established their reputation, and have a strong hold on the market. Without a price advantage, companies that wish to join the market for that product would have to be innovative, and offer better and improved features rather than just copying what is already offered, and this would promote competition. It is then up to the originators to keep one step ahead with a program of continuous improvement, which would be, to the benefit of the customer.

SUMMARY OF BENEFITS

In this chapter, I will summarise the more certain and tangible benefits of The Fair Dinkum Economy which have been discussed previously. I have not included the side-benefits of the effect on population control, world peace, foreign exchange, inflation and patents as they are less certain—any improvement in these areas would be an enormous bonus if they should eventuate.

To the Developing Countries:

- They would get a much better price for their exports, but they would have to improve the quality of their produce in order to meet the new international standards. This would mean a greater emphasis on research and product development, and encourage continuous improvement programs.
- Higher prices would mean they would be able to afford to increase the wages they pay to their workers, and upgrade their equipment and facilities.

- If they wish to continue exporting, these countries would have to improve their educational standards, and their companies would have to provide better training to their employees.
- Competition for skilled workers would mean companies would have to provide safer working conditions to attract good staff.
- I believe this would be the fastest way to increase the standard of living in these countries.

<u>To the Developed Countries:</u>

- Local producers would become price competitive with businesses overseas. This would lead to a re-growth of previously declining industries, particularly in manufacturing and agriculture.
- There would be a greater emphasis on quality and service which would be terrific for consumers.
- It would result in more stable, long-term contracts. This would give companies greater certainty and confidence to invest in their future.
- Skilled workers would be able to retain their jobs, and not have to re-train. This would stop valuable skills from being lost.
- Small business would be buying supplies and selling to customers at the same price as larger ones, which would result, in fairer competition, and a lower rate of business failure.
- Governments would be able to reduce the amount of financial assistance they provide to businesses.

- Traditional retail businesses would be better protected from the threat of online trading.
- It would halt the loss of valuable skills (e.g. farm and manufacturing workers).
- There would be a dramatic reduction in the amount of junk mail and an improvement in the quality of product information provided by sellers.
- Loan defaults would decrease, both company and personal.
- Hopefully it would change the attitude of business to their employees, and make them rethink their policies in regards to the distribution of their wealth.
- They would be able to maintain their existing standards of living.

To all countries:

- Estimating and tendering costs would be substantially reduced.
- There would be less impulse buying.
- There would be a substantial improvement in quality, things would be built to last and better perform.
- Items would be worth repairing rather than replacing.
- Food would start to taste better, and be better for us.
- Transportation would be reduced.
- It would help decentralisation.
- Farmers would be protected from the vagaries of the weather.

To the environment:

- Primary producers in all countries would receive a price for their produce, which would allow them, to rotate crops, minimise the use of fertilisers and herbicides, protect against loss of top soil, have sustainable fishing industries, and replace forests.
- Secondary industries would be able to invest in systems to minimise emissions, and dispose of waste product in a responsible manner.
- There would be less waste and landfill.
- It would extend the life of fossil fuels and non-renewable resources.

CONCLUSION

When you study the history of companies in Developed Countries you will see that Capitalism is truly a story of creation and destruction. The destructive stage is indeed terribly expensive and wasteful for both the owners/shareholders and the economy as a whole. There is no reason why companies cannot last for 200 years or for that matter, forever. If we can come up with a better system we should jump at it—the potential benefits are enormous. What I have suggested is a radical change; the decision to implement, will take a lot of courage. The decision to stay with the status quo (the current system) will be the easy option for those in power, but are they willing to accept responsibility for the consequences?

The influential economists of the 19th Century such as Engels, Marx, Mills, Smith, and Marshall differed in their opinions as to how to run an economy. Some favoured a free-market; some had the opposite view that substantial government control was essential while others had opinions involving varying degrees of regulation. However they all agreed on one thing, the market was a very complicated place which would be extremely difficult or impossible (depending on the theory) to control.

By the time the 20th Century came around, a number of these theories had been tested with varying degrees of success, but no one theory had been proven to be the best. The last 100 years have been mostly influenced by three economic giants, Keynes, Hayek, and Friedman. Hayek promoted the benefits of the free-market whilst the others supported some government regulation. Countries have largely used quick and easy methods to try and manipulate the market such as the changing interest rates, funding more public projects, increasing taxes or aiding industry to boost activity in times of recession. This interference has only made things worse; we are still in a mess, enduring never ending cycles of boom and bust, so the jury is still sitting waiting for more proof.

In the 21st Century things have changed radically which has opened up new opportunities, which were not available to these masterminds. The situation can be likened to comparing the opinions of two agricultural experts, one in 1920, and one in 2013, how different would their advice be when you consider the advances in tractors, automated equipment, fertilisers, pest control, irrigation, harvesting, plant and animal breeding, and the unravelling of the DNA puzzle which have occurred over that time period.

My suggestion of minimum price regulation would be complex to implement, but we now have the tools to make it possible. It is based on mathematics, and the benefits are tangible as opposed to the unpredictability of say lowering interest rates.

It would require a substantial amount of government control, but it would still allow the free-market and capitalism to operate unfettered, above a certain level. I feel that by limiting the degree of freedom, we would get the benefit of competition, without the disadvantages of the current system that I have highlighted in this book. By changing the emphasis from price to quality, we would encourage business to focus on continuous improvement which would increase their productivity, and this would lead to increased profits, wages, and the general standard of living in all countries. Consumers would have more say under The Fair Dinkum Economy, and companies would be held more accountable.

It is time to do some long-term planning for the future of our World, and to build things to last. Do we want to be remembered by our descendants as the selfish generations that wasted the World's resources! There are many influential people in society who will not want things to change, they are benefiting too much from the current arrangement. They would strongly oppose those who seek to bring about radical change and increased regulation. I think these people have blinkers on if they can't see what is happening to the foundations of our society and economy, and they will suffer along with everyone else if something is not done to address the problems.

So if you are like me, and not one of the great decision makers of this Planet you are probably thinking by now, "alright I agree the current system is far from perfect", and hopefully you are thinking, "what he is proposing seems to make sense and has merit, but what can I do to change it"? If you feel strongly enough about something you can make a difference no matter who you are. There is power in numbers, if enough people care, if enough people write to their newspapers, if enough people talk amongst themselves, if enough people talk to their politicians, and get behind this movement then I am hopeful, that eventually, it will be discussed in the halls of parliaments, and slowly it will happen.

Technology has given a real voice to the man on the street. We are at the threshold of rapid change in politics; up to now we have voted for representatives who promised to support our causes, but all too often, we have been disappointed. We are now seeing the Internet being used for opinion polls and as a forum to seek our suggestions in many fields. In the near future, I believe the election of our politicians will be done by voting via the Internet, and political parties will seek the approval of their constituents before passing changes to laws. Cloud computing and social media have given us the means to share our opinions quickly and easily, and we should take advantage of this to make ourselves heard and bring about the changes, which I believe, are needed.

Under my proposals, in Developed Countries in the short term, prices would increase. This would mean that consumers would not be able have as many material possessions as they do now, BUT what they would have would be guaranteed to last longer and give greater satisfaction. The alternative is to continue the way we are; if we do this then I predict buying power will decrease anyway as our economy and standard of living declines.

There are sure to be some, or maybe many out there, who strongly disagree with my ideas. I am aware the system I am proposing is far from complete. It would take a lot of effort from many people to make it workable. I ask you to open your mind and get involved. I hope this book will start people thinking along new lines about possibilities, and that maybe, just maybe, we can set a course which will see us safely through this storm.

Thanks for taking the time to share my thoughts.

ADDENDUM— OTHER EXAMPLES

It is the small things that annoy me, but not usually enough to make me complain. Over the last 10 years, I have seen hundreds of examples of poor quality goods that have failed to meet promises and expectations. I did not want to clutter my book with all these examples, so I have just included some of the poignant ones in the previous chapters. For those of you who may be interested, or still need some more convincing of the need for change, here are a few more examples which I am sure you will be able to relate to if you delve back into your memory:-

- How many umbrellas have you owned over the last 20 years?
- My son has a small business which uses a lot of electronic parts, many of which he can only source from overseas. He bought a control box last year, and when he inspected the item the heat-sink in the control box had no insulation. This could have caused a serious accident if he had not noticed it.

- It cost me nearly as much to buy a replacement glass jug for our coffee machine than it did to buy a new machine.

- My friend, Andrew, had a bearing go in his 2 year old clothes dryer. He said it would not be worth paying to get it repaired. Fortunately he was handy enough to install a new part himself. The new bearing only cost a few dollars, but it took him 2 hours by the time he bought the part, and did the work. How hard would it have been, and how much extra would it have cost, for the manufacturer to have just used a better quality bearing in the first place.

- My daughter just bought a small occasional table from one of the largest retailers in Australia for the bargain price of $39. It was one of those which required assembly, but when she got it home there was one part missing, a small plastic spacer which helped hold the glass top in place, it would have cost about 10cents to make. She rang the store, and was told "to return it for replacement". It was a 26 km round trip. We made sure to check the new one before we left the store. She had already partially assembled the table before she realised a part was missing; the time lost in doing this, disassembling and re-packaging the item for return was 40 minutes. The total extra cost was 2 hours of her time and $6 in car running expenses. The table was not the bargain she thought it would be.

- My wife bought me some new underpants when we were on holidays, yes they were cheap, made in China, I couldn't see much point (up till then) of spending a lot of money on something that no one will see other than the two of us. Anyway as we were on holidays, by the time I opened the packet we were 500 kilometres away, so I couldn't return them. The manufacturers had skimped on the material, they were the same style that I always buy, but there was only about 60% of the material—I had to be careful when dressing! Even though, they were the most uncomfortable ones I have ever had, I did not throw them out—it must be my Scottish blood. They sit in the bottom of my drawer, and only get used once I have exhausted all my other options.

- I bought my first pair of glasses 2 years ago, they cost $400, most of the cost was in the frame. I did not appreciate how good they were until I went to buy my second pair two years later, I only use them for reading, so I decided to save a few dollars (quite a few, I should have known better), and went for a special deal offered by a national chain of optometrist 2 pairs for $199— boy was I sorry! I could only read clearly when the text was in the exact middle of the lens, if I raised or lowered my head even a centimetre the text started to blur. I complained about this, but was told to persevere, and that I would get used to it—well I am still waiting, I can't wear them for more than 30 minutes before my eyes start to ache.

- I bought a packet of hooks of different shapes and sizes for hanging things in my garage, they came with screws. When I tried to screw them into the hardwood beams the screws snapped as soon as any decent pressure was applied. I couldn't get the ends of the screws out, so I had to drill new holes, and use some better quality screws that I had as spares. So I ended up with the first hook in a less than my ideal position. I threw out the rest of the dodgy screws.

- A couple of years ago I bought a fleecy jacket made in China (it is hard to find any that aren't made there or in India or Fiji). I examined it carefully, tried it on, and it looked good, but what I did not realise until I got it home was the sleeves were so snug around my wrist (come on I am an accountant I don't have thick limbs), that I could not wear a winter shirt or my watch underneath. It is also sitting in my wardrobe, rarely worn.

- I bought a good brand of the pod-type coffee maker 6 months ago. It has a separate jug for frothing the milk which has just broken.

- Whatever happened to zips that used to last the life of the garment? In the last 2 years, I have had zips fail on two pairs of pants and a jacket that were less than 2 years old, a 3 year old backpack and a 12 month old briefcase. In 1983, I bought a top quality European day backpack for bush walking. Despite plenty of use, it is still as good as the day I bought it other than being faded and not as waterproof. There are no holes or fraying of material, the stitching is intact and the zips still work as new. It has outlasted twelve cheap packs (made in Developing Countries) that we have bought since then for our children, for work and for shopping, so it is possible to make things last, even those subject to a hard life.

- My wife likes to wear different shoes to match her clothes (after all she is a woman). We can't afford to buy good quality shoes all the time, so often these cost under $60. They don't last too long, at best under two years and some under 6 months. It is either the stitching or buckles on the straps that go or the sole starts to peel off.

- You can buy an acoustic guitar for $50 (not the toy ones), but why would you want to! It would sound very ordinary, it would go out of tune quickly, and it would be hard to play. A good guitar has strings that are closely and evenly spaced from the frets which make it a joy to play, the tensioning keys stay put, so it stays in tune longer, and the case is made of quality wood for a rich sound—worth every penny of the $400 it would cost.

- Last year I bought a new, top-brand, laptop computer. When I got it home I loaded all the applications I had bought. The next day I realised the battery had not charged. I took it back; there was no apology they just gave me a new battery. I plugged it in overnight and still no charge so, back to the store again. They tested the charger, and eventually decided it was a fault in the computer. They gave me another computer and changed over the hard drive to save me having to reload my applications. This caused problems with my licences as the computer numbers did not match. I eventually had to reload all my software anyway to solve the problem.

- In 2010, I was given an IPOD/radio player for my birthday. It was a cheaper brand, not my choice! It was fine for the first 16 months then the digital volume button stopped working.

- The video board played up on the desktop computer I bought in 2007. Fortunately it was within the warranty period. The manufacturer sent someone out to replace it—good service, but unfortunately, the new board also stopped working about 9 months later.

- I was just at my son's place; his flimsy, 2 year old garden sprinkler has a plastic base with a significant crack which will render the whole thing useless once it breaks off.
- The same son has a 2 year old coffee maker, a middle of the range model, which has now broken down for the second time. The first time was after 18 months, and he had to spend $ 100 buying a new seal and replacing a knob that broke, doing the labour himself. This time he is just going to replace it.
- Six months ago I bought an E-Reader. I could not find the one I wanted in the shops, so I bought it from an Australian web site. On only the second day, I had trouble opening a book, and had to reboot the device to fix it. At first I thought that I must have done something wrong, but when it kept happening I realised the fault was not mine. It finally stopped completely last week. I will be interesting to see how I go getting it repaired.

I had better stop, I am depressing myself remembering!

N.B. These are examples from the experiences of just me, my family and a few friends, and they only cover about one quarter of the problems we have had over the last 5 years. Imagine how many problems there would be across the World.